THE COLD WAR
A DOCUMENTARY SURVEY

William Tilchin

Michael Kort

John Zawacki

Boston University

Learning Solutions

Boston   Burr Ridge, IL   Dubuque, IA   New York   San Francisco   St. Louis
Bangkok   Bogotá   Caracas   Lisbon   London   Madrid
Mexico City   Milan   New Delhi   Seoul   Singapore   Sydney   Taipei   Toronto

THE COLD WAR
A DOCUMENTARY SURVEY
FIFTH EDITION

2 3 4 5 6 7 8 9 0   DIG   DIG 14 13 12

ISBN-13: 978-0-07-811946-0
ISBN-10: 0-07-811946-4

Learning Solutions Consultant: Jessica Watts
Production Editor: Jennifer Pickel
Cover Photos Top Row:
   LIBRARY OF CONGRESS, PRINTS AND PHOTOGRAPHS DIVISION: Prime Minister Winston Churchill at Yalta LC-USZ62-7449 DLC; President John F. Kennedy LC-USZ62-117124 DLC; President Richard M. Nixon LC-USZ62-13037 DLC; President Ronald Reagan LC-USZ62-13040 DLC.
   U.S. NATIONAL ARCHIVES, ARMY SIGNAL CORPS COLLECTION: President Harry Truman en route to Potsdam.
Cover Photos Bottom Row:
   LIBRARY OF CONGRESS, PRINTS AND PHOTOGRAPHS DIVISION: Marshal Joseph Stalin, Soviet Leader at Yalta LC-USZ62-7449 DLC; Chairman Mao Zedong/©INGRAM PUBLISHING; Soviet Leader Nikita Khrushchev/AFP/GETTY IMAGES; Soviet Leader Leonid Brezhnev/© SUPERSTOCK, INC.; Soviet President Mikhail Gorbachev/© JACK NOVAK/SUPERSTOCK.
Cover Design: Fairfax Hutter
Printer/Binder: Digital Impressions

Table of Contents

I

WORLD WAR II AND THE ONSET OF THE COLD WAR

CHARTER OF THE UNITED NATIONS
signed in San Francisco on April 25, 1945

WE THE PEOPLES OF THE UNITED NATIONS DETERMINED

to save succeeding generations from the scourge of war, which twice in our lifetime has brought untold sorrow to mankind, and

to reaffirm faith in fundamental human rights, in the dignity and worth of the human person, in the equal rights of men and women and of nations large and small, and

to establish conditions under which justice and respect for the obligations arising from treaties and other sources of international law can be maintained, and

to promote the social progress and better standards of life in larger freedom,

AND FOR THESE ENDS

to practice tolerance and live together in peace with one another as good neighbors, and

to unite our strength to maintain international peace and security, and

to ensure, by the acceptance of principles and the institution of methods, that armed force shall not be used, save in the common interest, and

to employ international machinery for the promotion of the economic and social advancement of all peoples,

HAVE RESOLVED TO COMBINE OUR EFFORTS TO ACCOMPLISH THESE AIMS

Accordingly, our respective Governments, through representatives assembled in the city of San Francisco, who have exhibited their full powers found to be in good and due form, have agreed to the present Charter of the United Nations and do hereby establish an international organization to be known as the United Nations.

Source: U.S. Department of State, *Bulletin*, July 24, 1945, Vol. 12, p. 111a.

THE SPHERES OF INFLUENCE AGREEMENT
October 1944

On October of 1944 Winston Churchill and Anthony Eden traveled to Moscow and met with Marshal Stalin and his foreign minister, V. Molotov. No American representatives were present. This meeting, often referred to as the Moscow Conference, resulted in an important agreement known as the "Spheres of Influence Agreement." Much of what is known about this meeting between the two allies is based on Churchill's own memoir of the time and on British documents.

The purpose of the meeting was to discuss the degrees of influence the two governments would exercise over those parts of Eastern Europe and the Mediterranean which were considered vital to respective British and Soviet national interests.

Early in the conversations Churchill made it clear to Stalin that he accepted the border between Poland and the Soviet Union which had been discussed and approved at an earlier meeting in Teheran at which Roosevelt had been present. While Churchill agreed that the Soviets should exercise decisive control in Eastern Europe he maintained that the British required a similar role in those nations bordering the Mediterranean Sea, a critical link between the British Isles and those parts of its empire located in the Middle East and Asia. Churchill was determined that despite the toll exacted by the war on Britain's capabilities, the empire would remain intact. Churchill proposed a sort of trade in territory which he expressed in arithmetic terms: The Soviets would have a 90 per cent influence in Rumania; the British a 90 per cent influence in Greece; Yugoslavia would be shared equally as would Hungary; and Bulgaria would have a 75 per cent Soviet influence. Writing these percentages on a piece of paper, Churchill slid it across the table to Stalin who placed a bold "tic" mark in its corner.

The next day the two foreign ministers, Eden and Molotov, met to commit the percentages into a more permanent record. After considerable bargaining some minor adjustments were made to the initial deal. Greece and Rumania retained the original 90/10 split and Yugoslavia retained its equal division. However, the Hungarian and Bulgarian percentages were adjusted with the Soviets now enjoying an 80 per cent interest in both.

In a concrete sense these percentages meant that the dominant power would take the lead in organizing the new local government in each nation immediately upon the expulsion of the German Army. In Greece, for example, the British gave considerable assistance to the Royal Greek government in an effort to re-instate the Greek king who had fled when the Nazis invaded Greece early in the war. The 50/50 formula for Yugoslavia was designed to avoid a civil war between Serbs, Croats and Slovenes and to assist Marshal Tito to create a national government. As the World War ended to be replaced by the Cold War, local communists organized the governments in Eastern Europe with the substantial assistance of the Soviets.

Source: Resis, Albert, "The Churchill-Stalin 'Percentages' Agreement on the Balkans, Moscow, October 1944," *American Historical Review*, 83 (April 1978): 368–87.

U.S.–BRITISH–SOVIET AGREEMENTS OF THE YALTA CONFERENCE
February 1945

II. THE OCCUPATION AND CONTROL OF GERMANY

We have agreed on common policies and plans for enforcing the unconditional surrender terms which we shall impose together on Nazi Germany after German armed resistance has been finally crushed. These terms will not be made known until the final defeat of Germany has been accomplished. Under the agreed plan, the forces of the Three Powers will each occupy a separate zone of Germany. Coordinated administration and control has been provided for under the plan through a central Control Commission consisting of the Supreme Commanders of the Three Powers with headquarters in Berlin. It has been agreed that France should be invited by the Three Powers, if she should so desire, to take over a zone of occupation, and to participate as a fourth member of the Control Commission.

III. REPARATION BY GERMANY

We have considered the question of the damage caused by Germany to the Allied Nations in this war and recognize it as just that Germany be obliged to make compensation for this damage in kind to the greatest extent possible.

IV. UNITED NATIONS CONFERENCE

We are resolved upon the earliest possible establishment with our allies of a general international organization to maintain peace and security. We believe that this is essential, both to prevent aggression and to remove the political, economic and social causes of war through the close and continuing collaboration of all peace-loving peoples.

V. DECLARATION ON LIBERATED EUROPE

We have drawn up and subscribed to a Declaration on liberated Europe. This Declaration provides for concerting the policies of the three Powers and for joint action by them in meeting the political and economic problems of liberated Europe in accordance with democratic principles. The text of the Declaration is as follows:

> The Premier of the Union of Soviet Socialist Republics, the Prime Minister of the United Kingdom, and the President of the United States of America have consulted with each other in the common interests of the peoples liberated from the domina-

tion of Nazi Germany and the peoples of the former Axis satellite states of Europe to solve by democratic means their pressing political and economic problems.

The establishment of order in Europe and the rebuilding of national economic life must be achieved by processes which will enable the liberated peoples to destroy the last vestiges of Nazism and Fascism and to create democratic institutions of their own choice. This is a principle of the Atlantic Charter—the right of all peoples to choose the form of government under which they will live—the restoration of sovereign rights and self-government to those people who have been forcibly deprived of them by aggressor nations.

To foster the conditions in which the liberated peoples may exercise these rights, the three governments will jointly assist the people in any European liberated state or former Axis satellite state in Europe where in their judgement conditions require (a) to establish conditions of internal peace; (b) to carry out emergency measures for the relief of distressed people; (c) to form interim governmental authorities broadly representative of all democratic elements in the population and pledged to the earliest possible establishment through free elections of governments responsive to the will of the people; and (d) to facilitate where necessary the holding of such elections.

VI. POLAND

A new situation has been created in Poland as a result of her complete liberation by the Red Army. This calls for the establishment of a Polish Provisional Government which can be more broadly based than was possible before the recent liberation of western Poland. The Provisional Government which is now functioning in Poland should therefore be reorganized on a broader democratic basis with the inclusion of democratic leaders from Poland itself and from Poles abroad. This new Government should then be called the Polish Provisional Government of National Unity.

M. Molotov, Mr. Harriman and Sir A. Clark Kerr are authorized as a Commission to consult in the first instance in Moscow with members of the present Provisional Government and with other Polish democratic leaders from within Poland and from abroad, with a view to the reorganization of the present Government along the above lines. This Polish Provisional Government of National Unity shall be pledged to the holding of free and unfettered elections as soon as possible on the basis of universal suffrage and secret ballot. In these elections all democratic and anti-Nazi parties shall have the right to take part and to put forward candidates.

When a Polish Provisional Government of National Unity has been properly formed in conformity with the above, the Government of The U.S.S.R., which now maintains diplomatic relations with the present Provisional Government of Poland, and the Government of the United Kingdom and the Government of the United States will establish diplomatic relations with the new Polish Provisional Government of National Unity, and will exchange Ambassadors by whose reports the respective Governments will be kept informed about the situation in Poland.

The three Heads of Government consider that the eastern frontier of Poland should follow the Curzon Line with digressions from it in some regions of five to eight kilometers in favor of Poland. They recognize that Poland must receive substantial accessions of territory in the north and west. They feel that the opinion of the new Polish Provisional Government of National Unity should be sought in due course on the extent of these accessions and that the final delimitation of the western frontier of Poland should thereafter await the Peace Conference.

DISMEMBERMENT OF GERMANY

It was agreed that Article 12 (a) of the Surrender Terms for Germany should be amended to read as follows:

> "The United Kingdom, the United States of America and the Union of Soviet Socialist Republics shall possess supreme authority with respect to Germany. In the exercise of such authority they will take such steps, including the complete disarmament, demilitarization and dismemberment of Germany as they deem requisite for future peace and security."

REPARATION

The following protocol has been approved:

1. Germany must pay in kind for the losses caused by her to the Allied nations in the course of the war. Reparations are to be received in the first instance by those countries which have borne the main burden of the war, have suffered the heaviest losses and have organized victory over the enemy.

Source: *Foreign Relations of the United States: Diplomatic Papers. The Conference at Yalta*, Washington, 1945, pp. 968–84.

STALIN-HOPKINS CONVERSATION
May 26, 1945

Mr. Hopkins then said that a few days ago President Truman had sent for him and had asked him to come to Moscow to have a talk with Marshal Stalin.

Two months ago, Mr. Hopkins said, there had been overwhelming sympathy among the American people for the Soviet Union and complete support for President Roosevelt's policies which the Marshal knew so well. . . . The American people at that time hoped and confidently believed that the two countries could work together in peace as well as they had in war.

Prior to his departure, President Truman had expressed to him his great anxiety at the present situation and also his desire to continue President Roosevelt's policy of working with the Soviet Union and his intention to carry out in fact as well as in spirit all the arrangements, both formal and informal, which President Roosevelt and Marshal Stalin had worked out together.

Mr. Hopkins said that it was not simple or easy to put a finger on the precise reasons for this deterioration but he must emphasize that without the support of public opinion it would be very difficult for President Truman to carry forward President Roosevelt's policy. He said that the cardinal basis of President Roosevelt's policy which the American people had fully supported had been the concept that the interests of the U.S. were world-wide and not confined to North and South America and the Pacific Ocean.

Marshal Stalin replied that the reason for the failure on the Polish question was that the Soviet Union desired to have a friendly Poland, but that Great Britain wanted to revive the system of cordon sanitaire on the Soviet borders.

Mr. Hopkins replied that neither the Government nor the people of the U.S. had any such intention. . . . He stated that the U.S. would desire a Poland friendly to the Soviet Union and in fact desired to see friendly countries all along the Soviet borders.

Marshal Stalin said he would not attempt to use Soviet public opinion as a screen but would speak of the feeling that had been created in Soviet governmental circles as a result of recent moves on the part of the U.S. Government. He said these circles felt a certain alarm in regard to the attitude of the U.S. Government. It was their impression that the American attitude towards the Soviet Union had perceptibly cooled once it became obvious that Germany was defeated, and that it was as though the Americans were saying that the Russians were no longer needed. He said he would give the following examples:

(1) The question of the Reparations Commission. At Yalta, it had been agreed that the three powers would sit on this Commission in Moscow and subsequently the U.S. had insisted that France should be represented on the same basis as the Soviet Union. This he felt was an insult to the Soviet Union in view of the fact that France had concluded a separate peace with Germany and had opened the frontier to the Germans. . . . To attempt to place France on the same footing as the Soviet Union looked like an attempt to humiliate the Russians.

(2) The attitude of the U.S. Government towards the Polish question. He said that at Yalta it had been agreed that the existing government was to be reconstructed and that anyone with common sense could see that this meant that the present government was to form the basis of the new. He said no other understanding of the Yalta agreement was possible. Despite the fact that they were simple people the Russians should not be regarded as fools, which was a mistake the West frequently made, nor were they blind and could quite well see what was going on before their eyes. It was true that the Russians were patient in the interests of a common cause but their patience had its limits.

(3) The manner in which Lend-Lease had been curtailed. If the refusal to continue Lend-Lease was designed as pressure on the Russians in order to soften them up then it was a fundamental mistake.

Mr. Hopkins replied that what disturbed him most about the Marshal's statement was the revelation that he believed the U.S. would use Lend-Lease as a means of showing our displeasure with the Soviet Union. He wished to assure the Marshal that however unfortunate the impression this question had caused in the mind of the Soviet Government, he must believe that there was no attempt or desire on the part of the U.S. to use it as a pressure weapon.

Mr. Hopkins then said that with the Marshal's permission he would like to review the position of the U.S. in regard to Poland. He said the question of Poland per se was not so important as the fact that it had become a symbol of our ability to work out problems with the Soviet Union. He said that we had no special interests in Poland and no special desire to see any particular kind of government, that we would accept any government in Poland which was desired by the Polish people and was at the same time friendly to the Soviet Government. The Government and people of the U.S., Mr. Hopkins continued, were disturbed because the preliminary steps towards the re-establishment of Poland appeared to have been taken unilaterally by the Soviet Union together with the present Warsaw Government and that in fact the U.S. was completely excluded.

Marshal Stalin replied that he wished Mr. Hopkins would take into consideration the following factors: He said it may seem strange, although it appeared to be recognized in U.S. circles and Churchill in his speeches also recognized it, that the Soviet Government should wish for a friendly Poland. In the course of twenty-five years the Germans had twice invaded Russia via Poland. Thus Poland had served as a corridor for the German attacks on Russia. It was therefore in Russia's vital interest that Poland should be both strong and friendly. He said there was no intention on the part of the Soviet Union to interfere in Poland's internal affairs, that Poland would live under the parliamentary system, which is like Czechoslovakia, Belgium and Holland, that any talk of an intention to Sovietize Poland was stupid. He said even the Polish leaders, some of whom were communists, were against the Soviet system since the Polish people did not desire collective farms or other aspects of the Soviet system. In this the Polish leaders were right since the Soviet system was not exportable—it must develop from within on the basis of set conditions which were not present in Poland.

For this reason he fully recognized the right of the U.S. as a world power to participate in the Polish question and that the Soviet interest in Poland did not in any way exclude those of England and the U.S.

8

Stalin recalled that the Soviet Government had recognized the Warsaw Government and concluded a treaty with it at a time when their allies did not recognize this government. The need for these actions had arisen out of the presence of Soviet troops in Poland. The logic of the war against Germany had demanded that the Soviet rear be assured and the Lublin Committee had been of great assistance to the Red Army. He said it was contrary to the Soviet policy to set up a Soviet administration on foreign soil since this would look like occupation and be resented by the local inhabitants.

Mr. Hopkins said he would like to accent once again the reasons for our concern in regard to Poland, and indeed in regard to other countries which were geographically far from our borders. He said there were certain fundamental rights which, when infringed upon or denied, caused concern in the U.S. These were cardinal elements which must be presented if a parliamentary system is to be established and maintained. He said for example:

(1) There must be the right of freedom of speech, the right of assembly, the right of movement and the right to worship at any church that they desired.

(2) All political parties, except the fascist party and fascist elements, who represented or could represent democratic governments should be permitted the free use, without distinction, of the press, radio, meetings and other facilities of political expression;

(3) All citizens should have the right of public trial, defense by counsel of their own choosing, and the right of habeas corpus.

Marshal Stalin replied that these principles of democracy were well known and would find no objection on the part of the Soviet Government. He was sure that the Polish government, which in its declarations had outlined just such principles, would not only not oppose them, but welcome them. He said, however, that in regard to specific freedoms mentioned by Mr. Hopkins, they could only be applied in full in peacetime, and even then with certain limitations. He said, to sum up: (1) during time of war these political freedoms could not be enjoyed to the full extent, and (2) nor could they apply without reservations to fascist parties trying to overthrow the government.

Mr. Hopkins said that he must say rightly or wrongly that there was a strong feeling among the American people that the Soviet Union wished to dominate Poland. Hopkins "reminded Stalin again of the many minority groups in America who were not sympathetic to the Soviet Union" and told him very forcefully that he must "believe me when I told him that our whole relationship was threatened by the impasse on Poland." Stalin was adamant against release of the arrested Polish leaders, inveighed against British connivance with the Polish Government in Exile in London, and observed that "we must take into consideration Russian opinion as well as American opinion; that it was the Russian forces that had liberated Poland and if they had not gained the victory in Poland, with such a great loss of Russian life, nobody would be talking about a new Poland."

Source: Foreign Relations of the United States—Conference of Berlin (Potsdam), Vol 1, pp. 24 ff. Washington, D.C., Government Printing Office, 1960.

II

THE DECISION TO DROP
THE ATOMIC BOMBS

EXCERPTS FROM THE FRANK REPORT
June 12, 1945

I. PREAMBLE

The only reason to treat nuclear power differently from all the other developments in the field of physics is the possibility of its use as a means of political pressure in peace and sudden destruction in war. All present plans for the organization of research, scientific and industrial development, and publication on the field of nucleonics are conditioned by the political and military climate in which one expects those plans to be carried out.

In the past, science has often been able to provide also new methods of protection against new weapons of aggression it made possible, but it cannot promise such efficient protection against the destructive use of nuclear power. This protection can come only from the political organization of the world.

II. PROSPECTS OF ARMAMENTS RACE

It could be suggested that the danger of destruction by nuclear weapons can be avoided—at least as far as this country is concerned—either by keeping our discoveries secret for an indefinite time, or else by developing our nucleonic armaments at such a pace that no other nation would think of attacking us from fear of overwhelming retaliation.

The answer to the first suggestion is that although we undoubtedly are at present ahead of the rest of the world in this field, the fundamental facts of nuclear power are a subject of common knowledge. British scientists know as much as we do about the basic wartime progress of nucleonics.

In Russia, too, the basic facts and implications of nuclear power were well understood in 1940, and the experience of Russian scientists in nuclear research is entirely sufficient to enable them to retrace our steps within a few years, even if we should make every attempt to conceal them.

It may be asked whether we cannot prevent the development of military nucleonics in other countries by a monopoly on the raw materials of nuclear power. The answer is that even though the largest now known deposits of uranium ores are under the control of powers which belong to the "western" group, . . . the old deposits in Czechoslovakia are outside this sphere. . . .

We now consider the second of the two suggestions made at the beginning of this section, and ask whether we could not feel ourselves safe in a race of nuclear armaments by virtue of our greater industrial potential. . . .

However, such a quantitative advantage in reserves of bottled destructive power will not make us safe from sudden attack. Just because a potential enemy will be afraid of being "outnumbered and outgunned," the temptation for him may be overwhelming to attempt a sudden unprovoked blow. In no other type of warfare does the advantage lie so heavily with the aggressor.

III. PROSPECTS OF AGREEMENT

From this point of view, the way in which the nuclear weapons now being secretly developed in this country are first revealed to the world appears to be of great, perhaps fateful, importance.

One possible way—which may particularly appeal to those who consider nuclear bombs primarily as a secret weapon developed to help win the Present war—is to use them without warning on an appropriately selected object in Japan. . . . If we consider international agreement on total prevention of nuclear warfare as the paramount objective, and believe that it can be achieved, this kind of introduction of atomic weapons to the world may easily destroy all our chances of success. Russia, and even allied countries which bear less mistrust of our ways and intentions, as well as neutral countries, may be deeply shocked. It may be very difficult to persuade the world that a nation which was capable of secretly preparing and suddenly releasing a weapon as indiscriminate as the rocket bomb and a million times more destructive, is to be trusted in its proclaimed desire of having such weapons abolished by international agreement.

It must be stressed that if one takes the pessimistic point of view and discounts the possibility of an effective international control over nuclear weapons at the present time, then the advisability of an early use of nuclear bombs against Japan becomes even more doubtful—quite independently of any humanitarian considerations. If an international agreement is not concluded immediately after the first demonstration, this will mean a flying start toward an unlimited armaments race. If this race is inevitable, we have every reason to delay its beginning as long as possible in order to increase our head start still further.

Source: Reprinted with permission from "A Report to the Secretary of War—June, 1945," *Bulletin of the Atomic Scientist.* Vol. 1, May 1, 1946, pp. 2–4, 16. Copyright © 1946 by the Educational Foundation for Nuclear Science, Chicago, IL.

RECOMMENDATIONS ON THE IMMEDIATE USE OF NUCLEAR WEAPONS
June 16, 1945

SCIENCE PANEL • TOP SECRET

You have asked us to comment on the initial use of the new weapon. This use, in our opinion, should be such as to promote a satisfactory adjustment of our international relations. At the same time, we recognize our obligation to our nation to use the weapons to help save American lives in the Japanese war.

(1) To accomplish these ends we recommend that before the weapons are used not only Britain, but also Russia, France and China be advised that we have made considerable progress in our work on atomic weapons, that these may be ready to use during the present war, and that we would welcome suggestions as to how we can cooperate in making this development contribute to improved international relations.

(2) The opinions of our scientific colleagues on the initial use of these weapons are not unanimous: they range from the proposal of a purely technical demonstration to that of the military application best designed to induce surrender. Those who advocate a purely technical demonstration would wish to outlaw the use of atomic weapons, and have feared that if we use the weapons now our position in future negotiations will be prejudiced. Others emphasize the opportunity of saving American lives by immediate military use, and believe that such use will improve the international prospects, in that they are more concerned with the prevention of war than with the elimination of this specific weapon. We find ourselves closer to these latter views; we can propose no technical demonstration likely to bring an end to the war; we see no acceptable alternative to direct military use.

(3) With regard to these general aspects of the use of atomic energy, it is clear that we, as scientific men, have no proprietary rights. It is true that we are among the few citizens who have had occasion to give thoughtful consideration to these problems during the past few years. We have, however, no claim to special competence in solving the political, social and military problems which are presented by the advent of atomic power.

A.H. Compton
E.O. Lawrence
J.R. Oppenheimer
E. Fermi

[signed] J.R. Oppenheimer (For the Panel)

Source: Manhattan Engineer District Records, *Harrison-Bundy Files*, folder no. 76, National Archives, Washington, D.C., 1945.

RALPH BARD'S RESERVATION: MEMORANDUM ON THE USE OF ATOMIC BOMB
June 27, 1945

Ever since I have been in touch with this program I have had a feeling that before the bomb is actually used against Japan that Japan should have some preliminary warning for, say, two or three days in advance of use. The position of the United States as a great humanitarian nation and the fair play attitude of our people generally are responsible in the main for this feeling.

During recent weeks I have also had the feeling very definitely that the Japanese government may be searching for some opportunity which they could use as a medium of surrender. Following the three-power conference, emissaries from this country could contact representatives from Japan somewhere on the China Coast and make representations with regard to Russia's position and at the same time give them some information regarding the proposed use of atomic power, together with whatever assurances the President might care to make with regard to the Emperor of Japan and the treatment of the Japanese nation following unconditional surrender. It seems quite possible to me that this presents the opportunity which the Japanese are looking for.

I don't see that we have anything in particular to lose in following such a program. The stakes are so tremendous that it is my opinion that very real consideration should be given to some plan of this kind. . . .

Source: Manhattan Engineer District Records, *Harrison-Bundy Files*, Folder 70-77, National Archives, Washington, D.C., 1945.

GENERAL GROVES ON ALAMOGORDO ATOMIC BOMB TEST
July 18, 1945

This is not a concise, formal military report but an attempt to recite what I would have told you if you had been here on my return from New Mexico.

At 0530, 16 July 1945, the first full scale test was made of the implosion type atomic fission bomb. For the first time in history there was a nuclear explosion. And what an explosion!. . . . The bomb was not dropped from an airplane but was exploded on a platform on top of a 100-foot high steel tower.

The test was successful beyond the most optimistic expectations of anyone. Based on the data which it has been possible to work up to date, I estimate the energy generated to be in excess of the equivalent of 15,000 to 20,000 tons of TNT; and this is a conservative estimate. Data based on measurements which we have not yet been able to reconcile would make the energy release several times the conservative figure. There were tremendous blast effects. For a brief period there was a lighting effect within a radius of 20 miles equal to several suns at midday; a huge ball of fire was formed which lasted for several seconds. This ball mushroomed and rose to a height of over ten thousand feet before it dimmed. The light from the explosion was seen clearly at Albuquerque, Santa Fe, Silver City, El Paso and other points generally about 100 miles away. The sound was heard to the same distance in a few instances but generally to about 100 miles. Only a few windows were broken although one was some 125 miles away. A massive cloud was formed which surged and billowed upward with tremendous power, reaching the substratosphere at an elevation of 41,000 feet, 36,000 feet above the ground, in about five minutes, breaking without interruption through a temperature inversion at 17,000 feet which most of the scientists thought would stop it. Two supplementary explosions occurred in the cloud shortly after the main explosion. The cloud contained several thousand tons of dust picked from the ground and a considerable amount of iron in the gaseous form. Our present thought is that this iron ignited when it mixed with the oxygen in the air to cause these supplementary explosions.

With the assistance of the office of censorship we were able to limit the news stories. . . . In local papers one of these was a blind woman who saw the light.

Source: Foreign Relations of the United States: The Conference of Berlin (The Potsdam Conference, 1945), Washington, D.C., 1960, vol. 2, pp. 1361–68.

THE POTSDAM DECLARATION
BY THE HEADS OF GOVERNMENT, UNITED STATES, CHINA & THE UNITED KINGDOM
July 26, 1945

(1) We, the President of the United States, the President of the National Government of the Republic of China and the Prime Minister of Great Britain, representing hundreds of millions of our countrymen, have conferred and agree that Japan shall be given an opportunity to end this war.

(2) The prodigious land, sea and air forces of the United States, the British Empire and of China, many times reinforced by their armies and air fleets from the west, are poised to strike the final blows upon Japan. This military power is sustained and inspired by the determination of all the Allied nations to prosecute the war against Japan until she ceases to exist.

(3) The result of the futile and senseless German resistance to the might of the aroused free people of the world stands forth in awful clarity as an example to the people of Japan. The might that now converges on Japan is immeasurably greater than that which, when applied to the resisting Nazis, necessarily laid greater waste to the lands, the industry and the method of life of the whole German people. The full application of our military power, backed by our resolve, *will* mean inevitably the utter devastation of the Japanese homeland.

(4) The time has come for Japan to decide whether she will continue to be controlled by these self-willed militaristic advisers whose unintelligent calculations have brought the Empire of Japan to the threshold of annihilation, or whether she will follow the path of reason.

(5) Following are our terms. We will not deviate from them. There are no alternatives. We shall brook no delay.

(6) There must be eliminated for all time the authority and influence of those who have deceived and misled the people of Japan into embarking on world conquest, for we insist that a new order of peace, security and justice will be impossible until irresponsible militarism is driven from the world.

(7) Until such a new order is established and until there is convincing proof that Japan's war-making power is destroyed, points in Japanese territory to be designated by the Allies shall be occupied to secure the achievement of the basic objectives we are here setting forth. . . .

(10) We do not intend that the Japanese shall be enslaved as a race or destroyed as a nation, but stern justice shall be meted out to all war criminals, including those who

have visited cruelties upon our prisoners. The Japanese government shall remove all obstacles to the revival and strengthening of democratic tendencies among the Japanese people. Freedom of speech, of religion, and of thought, as well as respect for the fundamental human rights, shall be established. . . .

(13) We call upon the Government of Japan to proclaim now the unconditional surrender of all the Japanese armed forces, and to provide proper and adequate assurances of their good faith in such action. The alternative for Japan is prompt and utter destruction.

POTSDAM
July 26, 1945

Harry S. Truman
Winston S. Churchill
Approval of President Chiang Kai-shek

Source: *Foreign Relations of the United States: The Conference of Berlin (The Potsdam Conference)*, Washington, D.C., 1945, vol. 2, pp. 1474–76.

PRESIDENT TRUMAN'S ADDRESS
August 9, 1945

The British, Chinese and United States governments have given the Japanese people adequate warning of what is in store for them. We have laid down the general terms on which they can surrender. Our warning went unheeded; our terms were rejected. Since then the Japanese have seen what our atomic bomb can do. They can foresee what it will do in the future.

The world will note that the first atomic bomb was dropped on Hiroshima, a military base. That was because we wished in this first attack to avoid, insofar as possible, the killing of civilians. But that attack is only a warning of things to come. If Japan does not surrender, bombs will have to be dropped on her war industries, and, unfortunately, thousands of civilian lives will be lost. I urge Japanese civilians to leave industrial cities immediately, and save themselves from destruction.

I realize the tragic significance of the atomic bomb.

Its production and its use were not lightly undertaken by this Government. But we knew that our enemies were on the search for it. We know now how close they were to finding it. And we knew the disaster which would come to this nation, and to all peace-loving nations, to all civilization, if they had found it first.

That is why we felt compelled to undertake the long and uncertain and costly labor of discovery and production.

We won the race of discovery against the Germans.

Having found the bomb we have used it. We have used it against those who attacked us *without warning* at Pearl Harbor, against those who have starved and beaten and executed American prisoners of war, against those who have abandoned all pretense of obeying international laws of warfare. We have used it in order to shorten the agony of war, in order to save the lives of thousands and thousands of young Americans.

We shall continue to use it until we completely destroy Japan's power to make war. Only a Japanese surrender will stop us.

Source: Public Papers of the Presidents: Harry S. Truman, 1945, Washington, D.C., p. 212.

TRUMAN'S NAVY DAY SPEECH
October 27, 1945

Now we are in the process of demobilizing our naval force. We are laying up ships. We are breaking up aircraft squadrons. We are rolling up bases, and releasing officers and men. But when our demobilization is all finished as planned, the United States will still be the greatest naval power on earth. . . .

Why do we seek to reserve this powerful Naval and Air Force, and establish this strong Army reserve? Why do we need to do that? . . .

We . . . need this kind of armed might . . . for four principal tasks:

First, our Army, Navy and Air Force, in collaboration with our allies, must enforce the terms of peace imposed upon our defeated enemies.

Second, we must fulfill the military obligations which we are undertaking as a member of the United Nations Organization—to support a lasting peace, by force if necessary.

Third, we must cooperate with other American nations to preserve the territorial integrity and the political independence of the nations of the Western Hemisphere.

Fourth, in this troubled and uncertain world, our military forces must be adequate to discharge the fundamental mission laid upon them by the Constitution of the United States—to "provide for the common defense" of the United States.

These four military tasks are directed not toward war—not toward conquest—but toward peace. . . .

Let me restate the fundamentals of the foreign policy of the United States:

1. We seek no territorial expansion or selfish advantage. . . .
2. We believe in the eventual return of sovereign rights and self-government to all peoples who have been deprived of them by force. . . .
4. We believe that all peoples who are prepared for self-government should be permitted to choose their own form of government by their own freely expressed choice, without interference from any foreign source. That is true in Europe, in Asia, in Africa, as well as in the Western Hemisphere. . . .
6. We shall refuse to recognize any government imposed upon any nation by the force of any foreign power. In some cases it may be impossible to prevent forceful imposition of such a government. But the United States will not recognize any such government. . . .
12. We are convinced that the preservation of peace between nations requires a United Nations Organization composed of all the peace-loving nations of the world who are willing jointly to use force if necessary to ensure peace. . . .

The atomic bomb does not alter the basic foreign policy of the United States. . . .

We must find the answer to the problems created by the release of atomic energy—we must find answers to the many problems of peace—in partnership with all the peoples of the United Nations. For their stake in world peace is as great as our own. . . .

In our possession of this weapon, as in our possession of other new weapons, there is no threat to any nation. The world, which has seen the United States in two great recent wars, knows that full well. The possession in our hands of this new power of destruction we regard as a sacred trust. Because of our love of peace, the thoughtful people of the world know that that trust will not be violated, that it will be faithfully executed.

Indeed, the highest hope of the American people is that world cooperation for peace will soon reach such a state of perfection that atomic methods of destruction can be definitely and effectively outlawed forever.

Source: Public Papers of the Presidents, Harry S. Truman, 1945 (Washington, D.C.: 1960), pp. 431–38.

III

1946–1947:
TIME OF RISING TENSIONS

STALIN'S "ELECTION" SPEECH
February 9, 1946

. . .It would be wrong to think that the Second World War was a casual occurrence or the result of mistakes of any particular statesmen, though mistakes were undoubtedly made. Actually, the war was the inevitable result of the development of world economic and political forces on the basis of modern monopoly capitalism. Marxists have declared more than once that the capitalist system of world economy harbors elements of general crises and armed conflicts and that, hence, the development of world capitalism in our time proceeds not in the form of smooth and balanced progress but through crises and military catastrophes.

The fact is that the unevenness of development in the capitalist countries usually leads in time to violent disturbance of equilibrium in the world system of capitalism....

As regards the plans for a longer period ahead, the Party intends to organize a new mighty upsurge in the national economy, which would allow us to increase our industrial production, for example, three times over as compared with the prewar period. We must achieve a situation where our industry can produce annually up to 50,000,000 tons of pig iron [prolonged applause], up to 60,000,000 tons of steel [prolonged applause], up to 500,000,000 tons of coal [prolonged applause] and up to 60,000,000 tons of oil [prolonged applause]. Only under such conditions can we consider that our Motherland will be safe-guarded against all possible eventualities. [Stormy applause.] That will take three Five-Year Plans, I should think, if not more. But it can be done and we must do it. [Stormy applause.]

Source: Basil Dmytryshyn, *USSR: A Concise History*, 3rd edition (New York: Scribner's, 1978), pp. 459–67. Reprinted with permission of the author.

CHURCHILL'S "IRON CURTAIN" SPEECH
March 5, 1946

The United States stands at this time at the pinnacle of world power. It is a solemn moment for the American democracy. With primacy in power is also joined an awe-inspiring accountability to the future. . . .

We cannot be blind to the fact that the liberties enjoyed by individual citizens throughout the United States and British Empire are not valid in a considerable number of countries, some of which are very powerful. In these states, control is enforced upon the common people by various kinds of all-embracing police government, to a degree which is overwhelming and contrary to every principle of democracy. . . .

A shadow has fallen upon the scenes so lately lighted by the Allied victory. Nobody knows what Soviet Russia and its Communist international organization intends to do in the immediate future, or what are the limits, if any, to their expansive and proselytizing tendencies. I have a strong admiration and regard for the valiant Russian people and for my wartime comrade, Marshal Stalin. There is sympathy and good will in Britain—and I doubt not here also—towards the peoples of all the Russias and a resolve to persevere through many differences and rebuffs in establishing lasting friendships.

We understand the Russian need to be secure on her western frontiers from all renewal of German aggression. We welcome her to her rightful place among the leading nations of the world. . . .

From Stettin in the Baltic to Trieste in the Adriatic, an iron curtain has descended across the continent. Behind that line lie all the capitals of the ancient states of central and eastern Europe. Warsaw, Berlin, Prague, Vienna, Budapest, Belgrade, Bucharest and Sofia, all these famous cities and the population around them lie in the Soviet sphere and all are subject, in one form or another, not only to Soviet influence but to a very high and increasing measure of control from Moscow. . . .

Turkey and Persia are both profoundly alarmed and disturbed at the claims which are made upon them and at the pressure being exerted by the Moscow government. . . .

In front of the iron curtain which lies across Europe are other causes for anxiety. . . . The future of Italy hangs in the balance. Again, one cannot imagine a regenerated Europe without a strong France. . . .

However, in a great number of countries, far from the Russian frontiers and throughout the world, Communist fifth columns are established and work in complete unity and absolute obedience to the directions they receive from the Communist center. . . .

The outlook is also anxious in the Far East. In this country you all are so well informed about the Far East and such devoted friends of China that I do not need to expatiate on the situation there. . . .

Our difficulties and dangers will not be removed by closing our eyes to them; they will not be removed by mere waiting to see what happens; nor will they be relieved by a policy of appeasement. What is needed is a settlement, and the longer this is delayed, the more difficult it will be and the greater our dangers will become. From what I have seen of our Russian friends and allies during the war, I am convinced that there is nothing they admire as much as strength, and there is nothing for which they had less respect than military weakness. . . . If the Western democracies stand together in strict adherence to the principles of the United Nations Charter their influence for furthering their principles will be immense and no one is likely to molest them. If, however, they become divided or falter in their duty, and if these all-important years are allowed to slip away, then indeed catastrophe may overwhelm us all. . . .

There never was a war in all history easier to prevent by timely action than the one which has just desolated such great areas of the globe. . . .

We surely must not let that happen again. This can only be achieved by reaching, now, in 1946, a good understanding on all points with Russia under the general authority of the United Nations and by the maintenance of that good understanding through many peaceful years, by the world instrument, supported by the whole strength of the English-speaking world and all its connections.

Source: Congressional Record, 78th Congress, Second Session, 1946, pp. A 1145–47.

THE SOURCES OF SOVIET CONDUCT
by X
July 1947

The political personality of Soviet power as we know it today is the product of ideology and circumstances: ideology inherited by the present Soviet leaders from the movement in which they had their political origin, and circumstances of the power which they now have exercised for nearly three decades in Russia. . . .

The circumstances of the immediate post-revolution period—the existence in Russia of civil war and foreign intervention, together with the obvious fact that the Communists represented only a tiny minority of the Russian people—made the establishment of dictatorial power a necessity. . . .

But be that as it may, Stalin, and those whom he led in the struggle for succession to Lenin's position of leadership, were not men to tolerate rival political forces in the sphere of power which they coveted. Their sense of insecurity was too great. Their particular brand of fanaticism, unmodified by any of the Anglo-Saxon traditions of compromise, was too fierce and too jealous to envisage any permanent sharing of power. From the Russian-Asiatic world out of which they had emerged they carried with them a skepticism as to the possibilities of permanent and peaceful coexistence of rival forces....

Now the outstanding circumstance concerning the Soviet regime is that down to the present day this process of political consolidation has never been completed and the men in the Kremlin have continued to be predominantly absorbed with the struggle to secure and make absolute power which they seized in November 1917. They have endeavored to secure it primarily against forces at home, within Soviet society itself. But they have also endeavored to secure it against the outside world. For ideology, as we have seen, taught them that the outside world was hostile and that it was their duty eventually to overthrow the political forces beyond their borders. The powerful hands of Russian history and tradition reached up to sustain them in this feeling....

Now, it lies in the nature of the mental world of the Soviet leaders, as well as in the character of their ideology, that no opposition to them can be officially recognized as having any merit or justification whatsoever. Such opposition can flow, in theory, only from the hostile and incorrigible forces of dying capitalism. As long as remnants of capitalism were officially recognized as existing in Russia, it was possible to place on them, as an internal element, part of the blame for the maintenance of a dictatorial form of society. But as these remnants were liquidated, little by little, this justification fell away; and when it was indicated officially that they had been finally destroyed, it disappeared altogether. And this fact came to act upon the Soviet regime: since capitalism no longer existed in Russia and since it could not be admitted that there could be serious or widespread opposition to the Kremlin springing spontaneously from the liberated masses under its authority, it became necessary to justify the retention of the dictatorship by stressing the menace of capitalism abroad.

II

So much for the historical background. What does it spell in terms of the political personality of Soviet power as we know it today?

Of the original ideal, nothing has been junked. Belief is maintained in the basic badness of capitalism, in the inevitability of its destruction, in the obligation of the proletariat to assist in that destruction and to take power into its own hands. . . .

The first of these concepts is that of the innate antagonism between capitalism and Socialism. We have seen how deeply that concept has become imbedded in foundations of Soviet power.

This brings us to the second of the concepts important to contemporary Soviet outlook. That is the infallibility of the Kremlin. The Soviet concept of power, which permits no focal points of organization outside the Party itself, requires that the Party leadership remain in theory the sole repository of truth. For if truth were to be found elsewhere, there would be justification for its expression in organized activity. But it is precisely that which the Kremlin cannot and will not permit.

On the principle of infallibility there rests the iron discipline of the Communist Party. In fact, the two concepts are mutually self-supporting. Perfect discipline requires recognition of infallibility. Infallibility requires the observance of discipline. And the two together go far to determine the behaviorism of the entire Soviet apparatus of power. But their effect cannot be understood unless a third factor be taken into account: namely, the fact that the leadership is at liberty to put forward for tactical purposes any particular thesis which it finds useful to the cause at any particular moment and to require the faithful and unquestioning acceptance of that thesis by the members of the movement as a whole. This means that truth is not a constant but is actually created, for all intents and purposes, by the Soviet leaders themselves. . . .

But we have seen that the Kremlin is under no ideological compulsion to accomplish its purpose in a hurry. Like the church, it is dealing in ideological concepts which are of long-term validity, and it can afford to be patient. It has no right to risk the existing achievements of the revolution for the sake of vain baubles of the future. The very teachings of Lenin himself require great caution and flexibility in the pursuit of Communist purposes. Again, these precepts are fortified by the lessons of Russian history: of centuries of obscure battles between nomadic forces over the stretches of a vast unfortified plain. Here caution, circumspection, flexibility and deception are the valuable qualities; and their value finds natural appreciation in the Russian or the oriental mind. Thus the Kremlin has no compunction about retreating in the face of superior force. And being under the compulsion of no timetable, it does not get panicky under the necessity of such retreat. Its political action is a fluid stream which moves constantly, wherever it is permitted to move, toward a given goal. Its main concern is to make sure that it has filled every nook and cranny available to it in the basin of world power. But if it finds unassailable barriers in its path, it accepts these philosophically and accommodates itself to them. The main thing is that there should always be pressure, unceasing constant pressure, toward the desired goal. There is no trace of any feeling in Soviet psychology that the goal must be reached at any given time.

These considerations make Soviet diplomacy at once easier and more difficult to deal with than the diplomacy of individual aggressive leaders like Napoleon and Hitler. On the one hand it is more sensitive to contrary force, more ready to yield on individual sectors of the diplomatic front when that force is felt to be too strong, and thus more rational in the logic and rhetoric of power. On the other hand, it cannot be easily defeated or discouraged by a single victory on the part of its opponents. . . .

In these circumstances it is clear that the main element of any United States policy toward the Soviet Union must be that of a long-term, patient but firm and vigilant containment of Russian expansive tendencies. It is important to note, however, that . . . while the Kremlin is basically flexible in its reaction to political realities, it is by no means unamenable to considerations of prestige. Like almost any other government, it can be placed by tactless and threatening gestures in a position where it cannot afford to yield even though this might be dictated by its sense of realism. . . . For these reasons, it is *sine political non* of successful dealing with Russia that the foreign government in question should remain at all times cool and collected and that its demands on Russian policy should be put forward in such a manner as to leave the way open for a compliance not too detrimental to Russian prestige.

III

In the light of the above, it will be clearly seen that the Soviet pressure against the free institutions of the western world is something that can be contained by the adroit and vigilant application of counter-force at a series of constantly shifting geographical and political points, corresponding to the shifts and maneuver of Soviet policy, but which cannot be charmed or talked out of existence. . . .

Let us suppose that the western world finds the strength and resourcefulness to contain Soviet power over a period of ten to fifteen years. What does that spell for Russia itself?

The Soviet leaders, taking advantage of the contribution of modern technique to the arts of despotism, have solved the question of obedience within the confines of their power. Few challenge their authority; and even those who do are unable to make that challenge valid as against the organs of suppression of the state.

The Kremlin has also proved able to accomplish its purpose of building up in Russia, regardless of the interests of the inhabitants, an industrial foundation of heavy metallurgy, which is, to be sure, not yet complete but which nevertheless is continuing to grow and is approaching those of the other major industrial countries. . . . It has involved the neglect or abuse of other phases of Soviet economic life, particularly agriculture, consumer goods production, housing and transportation.

To all that, the war added its tremendous toll of destruction, death and human exhaustion. . . .

In these circumstances, there are limits to the physical and nervous strength of the people themselves. These limits are absolute ones, and are binding even for the cruelest dictatorship, because beyond them people cannot be driven. . . .

In addition to this, we have the fact that Soviet economic development, while it can list certain formidable achievements, had been precariously spotty and uneven. . . .

It is difficult to see how these deficiencies can be corrected at an early date by a tired and dispirited population working largely under the shadow of fear and compulsion. And as long as they are not overcome, Russia will remain economically a vulnerable, and in a certain sense an impotent, nation, capable of exporting its enthusiasms and of radiating the strange charm of its primitive political vitality but unable to back up those articles of export by the real evidences of material power and prosperity.

Meanwhile, a great uncertainty hangs over the political life of the Soviet Union. That is the uncertainty involved in the transfer of power from one individual or group of individuals to others.

This is, of course, outstandingly the problem of the personal position of Stalin. We must remember that his succession to Lenin's pinnacle of preeminence in the Communist movement was the only such transfer of individual authority which the Soviet Union has experienced. That transfer took 12 years to consolidate. It cost the lives of millions of people and shook the state to its foundation. The attendant tremors were felt all through the international revolutionary movement, to the disadvantage of the Kremlin itself. . . .

But this is not only a question of Stalin himself. There has been, since 1938, a dangerous congealment of political life in the higher circles of Soviet power. . . . Party mortality during the war was enormous; and today well over half of the Party members are persons who have matured since the last Party congress was held. Meanwhile, the same small group of men has carried on at the top through an amazing series of vicissitudes. . . .

It must be surmised from this that even within so highly disciplined an organization as the Communist Party there must be a growing divergence in age, outlook and interest between the great mass of Party members, only so recently recruited into the movement, and the little self-perpetuating clique of men at the top, whom most of these Party members have never met, with whom they have never conversed, and with whom they can have no political intimacy.

Who can say whether, in these circumstances, the eventual rejuvenation of the higher spheres of authority (which can only be a matter of time) can take place smoothly and peacefully. . . . And if disunity were ever to seize and paralyze the Party, the chaos and weakness of Russian society would be revealed in forms beyond description. . . .

If, consequently, anything were ever to occur to disrupt the unity and efficacy of the Party as a political instrument, Soviet Russia might be changed overnight from one of the strongest to one of the weakest and most pitiable of national societies.

IV

It is clear that the United States cannot expect in the foreseeable future to enjoy political intimacy with the Soviet regime. It must continue to regard the Soviet Union as a rival, not a partner, in the political arena. . . .

Balanced against this are the facts that Russia, as opposed to the western world in general, is still by far the weaker party, that Soviet policy is highly flexible, and that Soviet society may well contain deficiencies which will eventually weaken its own total potential. This would of itself warrant the United States entering with reasonable confidence upon a policy of firm containment, designed to confront the Russians with unalterable counterforce at every point where they show signs of encroaching upon the interests of a peaceful and stable world.

But in actuality the possibilities for American policy are by no means limited to holding the line and hoping for the best. It is entirely possible for the United States to influence by its actions the internal developments, both within Russia and throughout the international Communist movement, by which Russian policy is largely determined. This is not only a question of the modest measure of informational activity which this government can conduct in the Soviet Union, and elsewhere, although that, too, is important. It is rather a question of the degree to which the United States can create among the peoples of the world generally the impression of a country which knows what it wants, which is coping successfully with the problems of its internal life and with the responsibilities of a World Power, and which has a spiritual vitality capable of holding its own among the more ideological currents of our time. To the extent that such an impression can be created and maintained, the aims of Russian communism must appear sterile and quixotic, the hopes and enthusiasm of Moscow's supporters must wane, and added strain must be imposed on the Kremlin's foreign policies. . . .

By the same token, exhibitions of indecision, disunity and internal disintegration within this country have an exhilarating effect on the whole Communist movement. . . .

It would be an exaggeration to say that American behavior unassisted and alone could exercise a power of life and death over the communist movement and bring about the early fall of Soviet power in Russia. But the United States has it in its power to increase enormously the strains under which Soviet policy must operate, to force upon the Kremlin a far greater degree of moderation and circumspection than it has had to observe in recent years, and in this way to promote tendencies which must eventually find their outlet in either the break-up or the gradual mellowing of Soviet power. For no mystical, Messianic movement—particularly not that of the Kremlin—can face frustration indefinitely without eventually adjusting itself in one way or another to the logic of that state of affairs.

Thus the decision will really fall in large measure on this country itself. The issue of Soviet-American relations is in essence a test of the over-all worth of the United States as a nation among nations. To avoid destruction the United States need only measure up to its own best traditions and prove itself worthy of preservation as a great nation. . . .

Source: Reprinted by permission of *Foreign Affairs*, July 1947, pp. 566–82. Copyright © 1947 by the Council on Foreign Relations.

THE ROBERTS CABLES
March 1946

. . . There is one fundamental factor affecting Soviet policy dating back to the small beginnings of the Muscovite State. This is the constant striving for security of a state with no natural frontiers and surrounded by enemies. In this all-important respect the rulers and people of Russia are united by a common fear, deeply rooted in Russian history. National security is, in fact, at the bottom of Soviet, as of Imperial Russian, policy, and explains much of the high-handed behaviors of the Kremlin and many of the suspicions genuinely held there concerning the outside world. Russia has always been a more backward State than her neighbors. Even today the Soviet Union, despite its prestige in the world, is more backward than not only Britain or the United States, but also than most other European countries. She has grown around a small principality in Moscow, with no natural frontiers and always surrounded by unfriendly neighbors—Tartars, Poles, Turks, Teutonic Knights and Swedes. At the very birth of the new Soviet State the whole world seemed united against her, and the fears aroused by foreign intervention after 1917 cannot yet have been eradicated from the minds of the rulers of Russia. . . .

In all the greatest European crises since the French Revolution, Britain and Russia were brought together to fight against the domination of Europe by another Great Power, whether France or Germany. Now all that has changed. France is no longer a Great Power. Germany is at all events for the time being of no account. Austria-Hungary and the Turkish Empire no longer exist. The only other World Power is the United States, and there is clearly no reason why Britain and Russia should be brought to combine against her as a menace to their interest or to the peace of the world. Therefore Britain and Russia are now in immediate contact as never before, with no other Power to unite them in self-defense or act as a buffer between them. And between them there is now a greater ideological gulf than even in the 19th century. . . .

In this new situation, what is the Soviet attitude towards the outside world in general and Britain in particular? This is shown in the ideological line laid down for the Soviet public by the Communist party, since this not only conditions the thinking of the Soviet public but also guides the activities of the Communist parties throughout the world. This party teaching is not encouraging for the future of Anglo-Soviet cooperation. . . . The Western democracies, weak and disunited though they may be, are shown as the main dangers in a continued capitalist encirclement of the Soviet Union. . . .

In the light of these facts and of our recent experiences, one is driven to conclude not only that the rulers of the Soviet Union do not believe in the same things which Western democracies believe in, but that they are incapable of doing so. Reared as they have been in revolutionary traditions and impregnated with Marxist doctrine, they genuinely despise liberal ideas, tolerance, and the conceptions of right and justice which are the basis of Western thinking, however inadequately they may be interpreted in practice. The small group ruling Russia believe that the end justifies the means, and that they are at the head of a chosen people, or rather a chosen group of peoples, with a chosen system destined to spread throughout the world. In their view, relations with the outside world and even alliances are shorter arrangements for definite objectives, and can be modified or rejected as soon as they no longer suit the purpose of the Soviet Union. From Marxist-Lenin doctrine springs absolute confidence in the future of the Soviet State and system, deep suspicion and distrust of the outside world and complete disregard for all personal consideration and normal human relationships between individuals and States alike.

It is no use disguising the fact that the above situation is alarming. . . .

Any comparison between the German menace before the war and a Soviet menace today must also allow for the following fundamental differences:

a) In the first place, the Soviet Union, unlike Germany, is a vast territory containing all the primary products necessary for a modern State and with more than enough scope for all the energies of its peoples in developing these vast resources. . . .

b) Moreover, the rulers of Russia are infinitely more flexible than those of Germany. However much they may be wedded to Marxist doctrine, this allows them considerable latitude in regard of tactics and timing. Whereas the Germans set themselves a definite goal to be achieved within a given time regardless of opposition and changes in the international situation, the Russians are capable of readjusting their projects if faced by opposition or unexpected difficulties. . . .

c) Furthermore, the rulers of Russia have not got the same sense of urgency as Hitler, who knew that if Germany was to dominate Europe and the world she must act quickly.

d) Soviet Russia is also free from any sense of racial superiority or of a mission to dominate the world, though there is a certain Messianism in the Russian outlook. . . .

e) Finally, the internal position inside the Soviet Union, and in particular the economic structure, is at present much weaker than might be imagined if one listened to Soviet propaganda. The advent of the atomic bomb has shown that the Soviet military machine is by no means invincible, and the rulers of Russia know very well the inadequacy of the Red navy and air forces. They also know that there are strong forces throughout the world—American capitalism, British social democracy and the Catholic Church among them—which would form strong centers of opposition to any attempt by the Soviet Union in the immediate future to dominate the world. In fact, the Soviet Union, although confident of its ultimate strength, is nothing like so strong at present as the Western democratic world, and knows it. . . .

Basically, the Kremlin is now pursuing a Russian national policy which does not differ except in degree from that pursued in the past by Ivan the Terrible, Peter the Great or Catherine the Great. But what would, in other lands, be naked imperialism or power politics is covered by the more attractive garb of Marxist-Leninist ideology. . . .

In the first place every effort is being made to develop the Soviet Union into the most powerful State in the world, if necessary by its own unaided efforts, and meanwhile to provide for Soviet security. This means that at a time when other countries are busy demobilizing and reducing their armed forces, the Soviet Union is maintaining a very large military base, and hesitating even to reduce its garrison forces abroad, which probably number at least three million men. The search for security is a constantly expanding process. . . .

The second and connected objective is to weaken capitalist or social-democratic countries in every way. . . .

Everything possible will be done to keep the Americans and ourselves apart. . . .

Although the Communist International no longer exists, Communist parties everywhere will be supported and used to further Soviet interests, and ultimately to take over the government. . . .

Finally, and perhaps most important at the moment, the full weight of Soviet propaganda, and where possible active support, will be brought to bear in favor of the so-called oppressed colonial peoples and against imperial domination. This is in line with orthodox Marxist teaching, as well as with Soviet national interests. . . .

Source: Kenneth M. Jensen, editor, *Origins of the Cold War: The Novikov, Kennan and Roberts Long Telegrams* (Washington, D.C.: US Institute of Peace, 1991), pp. 34–56.

THE NOVIKOV TELEGRAM
Washington, September 27, 1946

...The foreign policy of the United States, which reflects the imperialist tendencies of American monopolistic capital, is characterized in the postwar period by a striving *for world supremacy*. . . .

The foreign policy of the United States is not determined at present by the circles in the Democratic party that (as was the case during Roosevelt's lifetime) strive to strengthen the cooperation of the three great powers that constituted the basis of the anti-Hitler coalition during the war. The ascendance to power of President Truman, a politically unstable person but with certain conservative tendencies, and the subsequent appointment of [James] Byrnes as Secretary of State, mean *a strengthening of the influence on U.S. foreign policy of the most reactionary circles of the Democratic party*. . . .

At the same time, there has been *a decline in the influence on foreign policy of those who follow Roosevelt's course for cooperation among peace-loving countries*. . . . *Wallace's resignation means the victory of the reactionary course* that Byrnes is conducting in cooperation with Vandenberg and Taft. . . .

Obvious indications of the U.S. effort to establish world dominance are also to be found in the increase in military potential in peacetime and in the establishment of a large number of naval and air bases both in the United States and beyond its borders. . . .

Expenditures on the army and navy have risen colossally, amounting to 13 billion dollars according to the budget for 1946–47 (about 40 percent of the total budget of 36 billion dollars). This is more than ten times greater than corresponding expenditures on the budget for 1938, which did not amount to even one billion dollars.

Along with maintaining a large army, navy and air force, the budget provides that these enormous amounts also will be spent on establishing a very extensive system of naval and air bases in the Atlantic and Pacific oceans. . . .

The establishment of American bases on islands that are often 10,000 to 12,000 kilometers from the territory of the United States and are on the other side of the Atlantic and Pacific oceans clearly indicates *the offensive nature of the strategic concepts* of the commands of the U.S. army and navy. . . .

All of these facts show clearly that a decisive role in the realization of plans for world dominance by the United States is played by its armed forces. . . .

Relations between the United States and England are determined by two basic circumstances. On the one hand, *the United States regards England as its greatest potential competitor*; on the other hand, *England constitutes a possible ally for the United States*. Division of certain regions of the globe into spheres of influence of the United States and England would create the opportunity, if not for preventing competition between them, which is impossible, than at least of reducing it. At the same time, such a division facilitates the achievement of economic and political cooperation between them. . . .

It is quite possible that the Near East will become *a center of Anglo-American contradictions* that will explode the agreements now reached between the United States and England.

The "hard-line" policy with regard to the USSR announced by Byrnes after the rapprochement of the reactionary Democrats with the Republicans is at present the main obstacle on the road to cooperation of the Great Powers. It consists mainly of the fact that in the postwar period the United States no longer follows a policy of strengthening cooperation among the Big Three (or Four) but rather has striven to undermine the unity of these countries. The *objective* has been to *impose* the will of other countries on the Soviet Union. . . .

The basic goal of this anti-Soviet campaign of American "public opinion" is to exert political pressure on the Soviet Union and compel it to make concessions. Another, no less important goal of the campaign is the attempt *to create an atmosphere of war psychosis* among the masses, who are weary of war, thus making it easier for the U.S. government to carry out measures for the maintenance of high military potential. . . .

Of course, all of these measures for maintaining a high military potential are not goals in themselves. They are only intended *to prepare the conditions for winning world supremacy* in a new war, the date for which, to be sure, cannot be determined by anyone, but which is contemplated by the most bellicose circles of American imperialism.

Careful note should be taken of the fact that the preparation by the United States for a future war is being conducted with the prospect of *war against the Soviet Union,* which in the eyes of American imperialists is the main obstacle in the path of the United States to world domination. . . .

Source: Kenneth M. Jensen, editor, *Origins of the Cold War.: The Novikov, Kennan and Roberts Long Telegrams* (Washington, D.C.: US Institute of Peace, 1991), pp. 3–16.

IV

FROM THE TRUMAN DOCTRINE TO NATO

DOCUMENT 1

THE TRUMAN DOCTRINE
PRESIDENT HARRY TRUMAN'S SPECIAL
MESSAGE TO THE CONGRESS ON
GREECE AND TURKEY
March 12, 1947

Mr. President, Mr. Speaker, Members of the Congress of the United States.

The gravity of the situation which confronts the world today necessitates my appearance before a joint session of the Congress.

The foreign policy and the national security of this country are involved.

One aspect of the present situation, which I wish to present to you at this time for your consideration and decision, concerns Greece and Turkey. . . .

When forces of liberation entered Greece they found that the retreating Germans had destroyed virtually all the railways, roads, port facilities, communications and merchant marine.

As a result of these tragic conditions, a militant minority, exploiting human want and misery, was able to create political chaos which, until now, has made economic recovery impossible.

The very existence of the Greek state is today threatened by the terrorist activities of several thousand armed men, led by communists, who defy the Government's authority at a number of points, particularly along the northern boundaries.

Meanwhile, the Greek Government is unable to cope with the situation. . . .

Greece must have assistance if it is to become a self-supporting and self-respecting democracy.

The United States must supply that assistance. . . .

There is no other country to which democratic Greece can turn.

No other nation is willing and able to provide the necessary support for a democratic Greek Government. . . .

No government is perfect. One of the chief virtues of democracy, however, is that its defects are always visible and under democratic process can be pointed out and corrected. The government of Greece is not perfect. . . .

The Greek Government has been operating in an atmosphere of chaos and extremism. It has made many mistakes. The extension of aid by this country does not mean the United States condones everything that the Greek Government has done or will do. We have condemned in the past, and we condemn now, extremist measures of the right or left. We have in the past advised tolerance, and we advise tolerance now. . . .

The future of Turkey as an independent and economically sound state is clearly no less important to the freedom-loving peoples of the world than the future of Greece. . . .

As in the case of Greece, if Turkey is to have the assistance it needs, the United States must supply it. We are the only country able to provide that help. . . .

One of the primary objectives of the foreign policy of the United States is the creation of conditions in which we and other nations will be able to work out a way of life free from coercion.

This is no more than a frank recognition that totalitarian regimes imposed on free peoples, by direct or indirect aggression, undermine the foundations of international peace and hence the security of the United States. . . .

At the present moment in the world's history nearly every nation must choose between alternative ways of life. The choice is too often not a free one.

One way of life is based upon the will of the majority and is distinguished by free institutions, representative government, free elections, guarantees of individual liberty, freedom of speech and religion, and freedom from political oppression.

The second way of life is based upon the will of the minority forcibly imposed upon the majority. It relies on terror and oppression, a controlled press and radio, fixed elections, and the suppression of personal freedoms. . . .

I believe that it must be the policy of the United States to support free peoples who are resisting attempted subjugation by armed minorities or by outside pressures.

It is necessary only to glance at a map to realize that the survival and integrity of the Greek nation are of grave importance in a much wider situation. If Greece should fall under the control of an armed minority, the effect upon its neighbor, Turkey, would be immediate and serious. Confusion and disorder might well spread throughout the entire Middle East.

Should we fail to aid Greece and Turkey in this fateful hour, the effect will be far-reaching to the West as well as to the East.

The seeds of totalitarian regimes are nurtured by misery and want. They spread and grow in the evil soil of poverty and strife. They reach their full growth when the hope of a people for a better life has died.

We must keep that hope alive.

The free peoples of the world look to us for support in maintaining their freedoms.

If we falter in our leadership, we may endanger the peace of the world—and we shall surely endanger the welfare of our own Nation.

Great responsibilities have been placed upon us by the swift movement of events.

Source: Public Papers of the Presidents of the United States: Harry S. Truman, 1947, Washington, D.C.: Government Printing Office, 1963, 176–80.

REMARKS BY SECRETARY OF STATE GEORGE C. MARSHALL AT HARVARD UNIVERSITY
June 5, 1947

I need not tell you gentlemen that the world situation is very serious. That must be apparent to all intelligent people. I think one difficulty is that the problem is one of such enormous complexity that the very mass of facts presented to the public by press and radio make it exceedingly difficult for the man in the street to reach a clear appraisal of the situation. Furthermore, the people of this country are distant from the troubled areas of the earth and it is hard for them to comprehend the plight and consequent reactions of the long-suffering peoples, and the effect of those reactions on their governments in connection with our efforts to promote peace in the world. . . .

In considering the requirements for the rehabilitation of Europe, the physical loss of life, the visible destruction of cities, factories, mines, and railroads [were] correctly estimated, but it has become obvious during recent months that this visible destruction was probably less serious than the dislocation of the entire fabric of European economy. For the past ten years conditions have been highly abnormal. The feverish preparation for war and the more feverish maintenance of the war effort engulfed all aspects of national economies. Machinery has fallen into disrepair or is entirely obsolete. Under the arbitrary and destructive Nazi rule, virtually.

For the past ten years conditions [in Europe] have been highly abnormal. The feverish preparation for war and the more feverish maintenance of the war effort engulfed all aspects of national economies. . . . Under the arbitrary and destructive Nazi rule, virtually every possible enterprise was geared into the German war machine. Long-standing commercial ties, private institutions, banks, insurance companies and shipping companies disappeared, through the loss of capital, absorption through nationalization or by simple destruction. In many countries, confidence in the local currency has been severely shaken. The breakdown of the business structure of Europe during the war was complete. . . . The rehabilitation of the economic structure of Europe quite evidently will require a much longer and greater effort than had been foreseen. . . .

The truth of the matter is that Europe's requirements for the next three or four years of foreign food and other essential products—principally from America—are so much greater than her present ability to pay that she must have substantial additional help, or face economic, social and political deterioration of a grave character.

The remedy lies in breaking the vicious circle and restoring the confidence of the European people in the economic future of their own countries and of Europe as a whole. The manufacturer and the farmer throughout wide areas must be able and willing to exchange their products for currencies the continuing value of which is not open to question.

Aside from the demoralizing effect on the world at large and the possibilities of disturbance arising as a result of the desperation of the people concerned, the consequences to the economy of the United States should be apparent to all. It is logical that the United States should do whatever it is able to do to assist in the return of normal economic health to the world, without which there can be no political stability and no assured peace. Our policy is directed not against any country or doctrine but against hunger, poverty, desperation and chaos. Its purpose should be the revival of a working economy in the world so as to permit the emergence of political and social conditions in which free institutions can exist. Such assistance, I am convinced, must not be on a piecemeal basis as various crises develop. Any assistance that this Government may render in the future should provide a cure rather than a mere palliative. Any government that is willing to assist in the task of recovery will find full cooperation, I am sure, on the part of the United States Government. Any government which maneuvers to block the recovery of other countries cannot expect help from us. Furthermore, governments, political parties or groups which seek to perpetuate human misery in order to profit therefrom politically or otherwise will encounter the opposition of the United States.

It is already evident that, before the United States Government can proceed much further in its efforts to alleviate the situation and help start the European world on its way to recovery, there must be some agreement among the countries of Europe as to the requirements of the situation and the part those countries themselves will take in order to give proper effect to whatever action might be undertaken by this Government. It would be neither fitting nor efficacious for this Government to undertake to draw up unilaterally a program designed to place Europe on its feet economically. This is the business of the Europeans. The initiative, I think, must come from Europe. The role of this country should consist of friendly aid in the drafting of a European program and of later support of such a program so far as it may be practical for us to do so. The program should be a joint one, agreed to by a number, if not all, European nations. . . .

An essential part of any successful action on the part of the United States is an understanding on the part of the people of America of the character of the problem and the remedies to be applied. Political passion and prejudice should have no part. With foresight, and a willingness on the part of our people to face up to the vast responsibility which history has clearly placed upon our country, the difficulties I have outlined can and will be overcome.

Source: *Foreign Relations of the United States, 1947, The British Commonwealth,* Vol. 3, 1972, 237–39.

MOLOTOV RESPONSE TO THE MARSHALL PLAN
July 2, 1947

The Soviet Government, considering the Anglo-French plan to set up a special organization for the co-ordination of the economies of European states would lead to interference in the internal affairs of European countries, particularly those which have the greatest need for outside aid, and believing that this can only complicate relations between countries of Europe and hamper their cooperation, rejects this plan as being altogether unsatisfactory and incapable of yielding any positive results.

On the other hand, the Soviet Union favors the fullest development of economic collaboration between European countries and other countries on a healthy basis of equality and mutual respect. . . .

What would the implementation of the Franco-British proposal concerning the setting up of a special organization or of a "steering committee" for the elaboration of a comprehensive European program lead to?

It would lead to no good results.

It would lead to Great Britain, France and that group of countries which follows them separating themselves from the other European states and thus dividing Europe into two groups of states and creating new difficulties in the relations between them.

In that case American credits would serve not to facilitate the economic rehabilitation of Europe, but to make use of some European countries against other European countries in whatever way certain strong powers seeking to establish their domination should find it profitable to do so.

The Soviet government considers it necessary to caution the governments of Great Britain and of France against the consequences of such action, which would be directed not toward the unification of the efforts of the countries of Europe in the task of their economic rehabilitation after the war, but would lead to opposite results, which have nothing in common with the real interests of the people of Europe.

Source: The New York Times, July 3, 1947.

ZHDANOV'S SPEECH AT THE FOUNDING OF THE COMINFORM
September 1947

The principal outcome of World War II was the military defeat of Germany and Japan—the two most militaristic and aggressive of the capitalist countries. The reactionary imperialist elements all over the world, notably in Britain, America and France, had reposed great hopes in Germany and Japan, and chiefly in Hitler: firstly as a force most capable of inflicting a blow on the Soviet Union in order to, if not having it destroyed altogether, weaken it at least and undermine its influence. . . .

But the hopes reposed by the British, French and American imperialists in the Hitlerites were not realized. . . .

The war immensely enhanced the international significance and prestige of the USSR. The USSR was the leading force and guiding spirit in the military defeat of Germany and Japan. The progressive democratic forces of the whole world rallied around the Soviet Union. The socialist state successfully stood the strenuous test of the war and emerged victorious from the mortal struggle with a most powerful enemy. Instead of being enfeebled, the USSR became stronger. . . .

World War II aggravated the crisis of the colonial system, as expressed in the rise of a powerful movement for national liberation in the colonies and dependencies. This has placed the rest of the capitalist system in jeopardy. . . .

But America's aspirations to world supremacy encounter an obstacle in the USSR, the stronghold of anti-imperialist and anti-fascist policy, and its growing international influence in the new democracies which have escaped from the control of British and American imperialism, and in the workers of all countries, including America itself, who do not want a new war for the supremacy of their oppressors. . . .

Alarmed by the achievements of Socialism in the USSR, by the achievements of the new democracies and by the post-war growth of the labor and democratic movement in all countries, the American reactionaries are disposed to take upon themselves the mission of "saviours" of the capitalist system from Communism. . . .

The Truman doctrine, which provides for rendering of American assistance to all reactionary regimes which actively oppose the democratic peoples, bears a frankly aggressive character. . . .

The vague and deliberately guarded formulations of the Marshall Plan amount in essence to a scheme to create a bloc of states bound by obligations to the United States, and to grant

American credits to European countries as a recompense for their renunciation of economic, and then political, independence. Moreover, the cornerstone of the Marshall Plan is the restoration of the industrial areas of Western Germany, controlled by the American monopolies. . . .

Source: Andre Zhdanov, *Report on the International Situation, at the Founding Conference of the Communist Information Bureau in Poland,* September 1947 (English translation in *The Strategy and Tactics of World Communism: Supplement I,* "One Hundred Years of Communism, 1848-1948" (U.S. House of Representatives Document No. 619, 80th Congress, 2nd Session), Washington, D.C., Government Printing Office, 1948, pp. 212–29.

NORTH ATLANTIC TREATY
April 1949

The Parties of this Treaty reaffirm their faith in the purposes and principles of the Charter of the United Nations and their desire to live in peace with all peoples and all governments.

They are determined to safeguard the freedom, common heritage and civilization of their peoples, founded on the principles of democracy, individual liberty and the rule of law.

They seek to promote stability and well-being in the North Atlantic area. They are resolved to unite their efforts for collective defense and for the preservation of peace and security.

They therefore agree to this North Atlantic Treaty:

ARTICLE 1

The Parties undertake, as set forth in the Charter of the United Nations, to settle any international disputes in which they may be involved by peaceful means in such a manner that international peace and security, and justice, are not endangered, and to refrain in their international relations from the threat or use of force in any manner inconsistent with the purposes of the United Nations.

ARTICLE 2

The Parties will contribute toward the further development of peaceful and friendly international relations by strengthening their free institutions, by bringing about a better understanding of the principles upon which these institutions are founded, and by promoting conditions of stability and well-being. They will seek to eliminate conflict in their international economic policies and will encourage economic collaboration between any or all of them.

ARTICLE 3

In order more effectively to achieve the objectives of this Treaty, the Parties, separately and jointly, by means of continuous and effective self-help and mutual aid, will maintain and develop their individual and collective capacity to resist armed attack.

ARTICLE 4

The Parties will consult together whenever, in the opinion of any of them, the territorial integrity, political independence or security of any of the Parties is threatened.

ARTICLE 5

The Parties agree that an armed attack against one or more of them in Europe or North America shall be considered an attack against them all; and consequently they agree that, if such an armed attack occurs, each of them, in exercise of the right of individual or collective self-defense recognized by Article 51 of the Charter of the United Nations, will assist the Party or Parties so attacked by taking forthwith, individually and in concert with the other Parties, such action as it deems necessary, including the use of armed force, to restore and maintain the security of the North Atlantic area.

ARTICLE 6

For the purpose of Article 5 an armed attack on one or more of the Parties is deemed to include an armed attack on the territory of any of the Parties in Europe or North America, on the Algerian departments of France, on the occupation forces of any Party in Europe, on the islands under the jurisdiction of any Party in the North Atlantic area north of the Tropic of Cancer or on the vessels or aircraft in this area of any of the Parties.

. . . .

ARTICLE 9

The Parties hereby establish a council, on which each of them shall be represented, to consider matters concerning the implementation of this Treaty.

ARTICLE 10

The Parties may, by unanimous agreement, invite any other European state in a position to further the principles of this Treaty and to contribute to the security of the North Atlantic to accede to this Treaty.

. . . .

ARTICLE 13

After the Treaty has been in force for twenty years, any Party may cease to be a party one year after notice of denunciation. . . .

Source: Foreign Relations of the United States, 1949, Western Europe, 1975, Vol. 4, pp. 281–84.

handwritten: Why Taft opposed Nato

ROBERT A. TAFT: OBJECTIONS TO THE NATO PACT
July 11, 1949

First. . . . The pact is a military alliance, a treaty by which one nation undertakes to arm half the world against the other half, and in which all the pact members agree to go to war if one is attacked. It cannot be described otherwise than a military alliance. . . .

While this is not an offensive alliance, the line between defense and offense today is indeed a shadowy one. The Maginot line was the essence of pure defense. Today it is the target of ridicule. Every good defense includes elements of offense. We cannot have an adequate armament for defense which cannot be converted overnight into a weapon of offense. We talked of defense for years before entering World War II while our preparation was really for offense. The result is, that no matter how defensive an alliance may be, if it carries the obligation to arm it means the building up of competitive offensive armament. This treaty, therefore, means inevitably an armament race and armament races in the past have led to war. The United Nations looks perhaps vainly to the reduction of armaments. The Atlantic Pact proposes to increase them.

Second. The pact standing by itself would clearly be a deterrent to war. If Russia knows that if it starts a war it will immediately find itself at war with the United States, it is much less likely to start a war. I see and believe in the full force of that argument. That is why I would favor the extension of the Monroe Doctrine to Europe. But if Russia sees itself ringed about gradually by so-called defensive arms from Norway and Denmark to Turkey and Greece, it may form a different opinion. It may decide that the arming of Western Europe, regardless of its present purpose, looks to an attack upon Russia. Its view may be unreasonable, and I think it is. But from the Russian standpoint it may not seem unreasonable. They may well decide that if war is the certain result, that war might better occur now rather than after the arming of Europe is completed. . . .

Third. The pact ... violates our obligations under the United Nations. . . .

An undertaking by the most powerful nation in the world to arm half the world against the other half goes far beyond any "right of collective self-defense if an armed attack occurs." It violates the whole spirit of the United Nations Charter. That Charter looks to the reduction of armaments by agreement between individual nations. I do not claim that there is any direct violation of the Charter, but the Atlantic Pact moves in exactly the opposite direction from the purposes of the Charter and makes a farce of further efforts to secure international peace through law and justice. It necessarily divides the world into two armed camps. It may be said that the world is already so divided, but it cannot be said that by enforcing that division we are carrying out the spirit of the United Nations.

Source: Congressional Record, 81st Congress, 1st Session, 1949, pp. 9208–10, abridged.

V

THE FAR EAST AND THE GLOBALIZATION OF THE COLD WAR

MARSHALL ON THE CHINA MISSION
January 7, 1947

The President has recently given a summary of the developments in China during the past year and the position of the American Government toward China. Circumstances now dictate that I should supplement this with impressions gained at first hand.

In the first place, the greatest obstacle to peace has been the complete, almost overwhelming suspicion with which the Chinese Communist Party and the Kuomintang regard each other.

On the one hand, the leaders of the government are strongly opposed to a communistic form of government. On the other, the Communists frankly state that they are Marxists and intend to work toward establishing a communistic form of government in China though first advancing through the medium of a democratic form of government of the American or British type.

The leaders of the Government are convinced in their minds that the Communist-expressed desire to participate in a government of the type endorsed by the Political Consultative Conference last January had for its purpose only a destructive intention. The Communists felt, I believe, that the government was insincere in its apparent acceptance of the PCC resolution for the formation of the new government and intended by coercion of military force and the action of secret police to obliterate the Communist Party. Combined with this mutual deep distrust was the conspicuous error by both parties of ignoring the effect of the fears and suspicions of the other party in estimating the reason for proposals or opposition regarding the settlement of various matters under negotiation. They each sought only to take counsel of their own fears. They both, therefore, to that extent took a rather lopsided view of each situation and were susceptible to every evil suggestion or possibility.

I think the most important factors involved in the recent breakdown of negotiations are these: On the side of the National Government, which is in effect the Kuomintang, there is a dominant group of reactionaries who have been opposed, in my opinion, to almost every effort I have made to influence the formation of a genuine coalition government. They were quite frank in publicly stating their belief that cooperation by the Chinese Communist Party in the government was inconceivable and that only a policy of force could definitely settle the issue. This group includes military as well as political leaders.

On the side of the Chinese Communist Party there are, I believe, liberals as well as radicals, though this view is vigorously opposed by many who believe that the Chinese Communist Party discipline is too rigidly enforced to admit of such differences of viewpoint. Nevertheless, it has appeared to me that there is a definite liberal group among the Communists, especially of young men who have turned to the Communists in disgust at the corruption evident in the local governments—men who would put the interest of the Chinese people above ruthless measures to establish a Communist ideology in the immediate future. The dyed-in-the-wool Communists do not hesitate at the most drastic measures to gain their end as, for instance, the destruction of communications in order to wreck the economy of China and produce a situation that would facilitate the overthrow or collapse of the government, without any regard to the immediate suffering of the people involved. They completely distrust the leaders of the Kuomintang and appear convinced that every government proposal is designed to crush the Chinese Communist Party. I must say that the quite evidently inspired mob actions of last February and March, some within a few blocks of where I was then engaged in completing negotiations, gave the Communists good excuse for such suspicion.

However, a very harmful and immensely provocative phase of the Chinese Communist Party procedures has been in the character of its propaganda. I wish to state to the American people that in the deliberate misrepresentation and abuse of the action, policies and purposes of our government this propaganda has been without regard for the truth, without any regard whatsoever for the facts, and has given plain evidence of a determined purpose to mislead the Chinese people and the world and to arouse a bitter hatred of Americans.

In the interest of fairness, I must state that the Nationalist Government publicity agency has made numerous misrepresentations, though not of the vicious nature of the Communist propaganda.

Source: U.S. Department of State, *United States Relations with China,* August, 1950, pp. 686–87.

SECRETARY OF STATE DEAN ACHESON'S SPEECH BEFORE THE NATIONAL PRESS CLUB
January 12, 1950

. . . What is the situation in regard to the military security of the Pacific area, and what is our policy in regard to it?

The defensive perimeter runs along the Aleutians to Japan and then goes to the Ryukyus. We hold important defense positions in the Ryukyu Islands, and those we will continue to hold. . . .

The defensive perimeter runs from the Ryukyus to the Philippine Islands. . . . It is hardly necessary for me to say an attack on the Philippines could not and would not be tolerated by the United States.

So far as the military security of other areas in the Pacific is concerned, it must be clear that no person can guarantee these areas against military attack.

Should an attack occur—one hesitates to say where such an armed attack could come from—the initial reliance must be on the people attacked to resist it and then upon the commitments of the entire civilized world under the Charter of the United Nations which so far has not proved a weak reed. . . .

In Korea we have taken steps which have ended our military occupation, and in cooperation with the United Nations, have established an independent and sovereign country recognized by nearly all the rest of the world. We have given that nation great help in getting itself established.

The idea that we should scrap all of that, that we should stop half way through the achievement of the establishment of this country, seems to me to be the most utter defeatism and utter madness in our interests in Asia.

Source: U.S. Department of State, *Bulletin*, Jan. 23, 1950, Washington, D.C. vol. 12, pp. 111–19.

McCARTHY ATTACKS THE STATE DEPARTMENT
February 12, 1950

Ladies and gentlemen, tonight as we celebrate the one hundred and forty-first birthday of one of the greatest men in American history, I would like to be able to talk about what a glorious day today is in the history of the world. As we celebrate the birth of this man who with his whole heart and soul hated war, I would like to be able to speak of peace in our time, of war being outlawed, and of world-wide disarmament. These would be truly appropriate things to be able to mention as we celebrate the birthday of Abraham Lincoln.

Five years after a world war has been won, men's hearts should anticipate a long peace, and men's minds should be free from the heavy weight that comes with war. But this is not such a period—for this is not a period of peace. This is a time of the "cold war." This is a time when all the world is split into two vast, increasingly hostile armed camps—a time of a great armaments race.

Today we can almost physically hear the mutterings and rumblings of an invigorated god of war. You can see it, feel it, and hear it all the way from the hills of Indochina, from the shores of Formosa, right over into the very heart of Europe itself.

The one encouraging thing is that the "mad moment" has not yet arrived for the firing of the gun or the exploding of the bomb which will set civilization about the final task of destroying itself. There is still a hope for peace if we finally decide that no longer can we safely blind our eyes and close our ears to those facts which are shaping up more and more clearly. And that is what we are now engaged in—a show-down fight—not the usual war between nations for land areas or other material gains, but a war between two diametrically opposed ideologies.

The great difference between our western Christian world and the atheistic Communist world is not political, ladies and gentlemen, it is moral. There are other differences, of course, but those could be reconciled. For instance, the Marxian idea of confiscating the land and factories and running the entire economy as a single enterprise is momentous. Likewise, Lenin's invention of the one-party police state as a way to make Marx's idea work is hardly less momentous.

Stalin's resolute putting across of these two ideas, of course, did much to divide the world. With only those differences, however, the East and the West could most certainly still live in peace.

The real, basic difference, however, lies in the religion of immoralism—invented by Marx, preached feverishly by Lenin, and carried to unimaginable extremes by Stalin. This religion of immoralism, if the Red half of the world wins—and well it may—this religion of immoralism will more deeply wound and damage mankind than any conceivable economic or political system. . . .

Today we are engaged in a final, all-out battle between communistic atheism and Christianity. The modern champions of communism have selected this as the time. And, ladies and gentlemen, the chips are down—they are truly down. . . .

Ladies and gentlemen, can there be anyone here tonight who is so blind as to say that the war is not on? Can there be anyone who fails to realize that the Communist world has said, "The time is now"—that this is the time for the show-down between the democratic Christian world and the Communist atheistic world?

Unless we face this fact, we shall pay the price that must be paid by those who wait too long.

Six years ago, at the time of the first conference to map out the peace—Dumbarton Oaks—there was within the Soviet orbit 180,000,000 people. Lined up on the antitotalitarian side there were in the world at that time roughly 1,625,000,000 people. Today, only 6 years later, there are 800,000,000 people under the absolute domination of Soviet Russia—an increase of over 400 percent. On our side, the figure has shrunk to around 500,000,000. In other words, in less than 6 years the odds have changed from 9 to 1 in our favor to 8 to 5 against us. This indicates the swiftness of the tempo of Communist victories and American defeats in the cold war.

As one of our outstanding historical figures once said, "When a great democracy is destroyed, it will not be because of enemies from without, but rather because of enemies from within." The truth of this statement is becoming terrifyingly clear as we see this country each day losing on every front.

At war's end we were physically the strongest nation on earth and, at lease potentially, the most powerful intellectually and morally. Ours could have been the honor of being a beacon in the desert of destruction, a shining living proof that civilization was not yet ready to destroy itself. Unfortunately, we have failed miserably and tragically to arise to the opportunity.

The reason why we find ourselves in a position of impotency is not because our only powerful potential enemy has sent men to invade our shores, but rather because of the traitorous actions of those who have been treated so well by this Nation. It has not been the less fortunate or members of minority groups who have been selling this Nation out, but rather those who have had all the benefits that the wealthiest nation on earth has had to offer—the finest homes, the finest college educations, and the finest jobs in Government we can give.

This is glaringly true in the State Department. There the bright young men who are born with silver spoons in their mouths are the ones who have been worst. . . .

When Chiang Kai-shek was fighting our war, the State Department had in China a young man named John S. Service. His task, obviously, was not to work for the communization of China. Strangely, however, he sent official reports back to the State Department urging that we torpedo our ally Chiang Kai-shek and stating, in effect, that communism was the best hope for China.

Later, this man—John Service—was picked up by the Federal Bureau of Investigation for turning over to the Communists secret State Department information. Strangely, however, he was never prosecuted. However, Joseph Grew, the Under Secretary of State, who insisted on his prosecution, was forced to resign. Two days after Grew's successor, Dean Acheson, took over as Under Secretary of State, this—John Service—who had been picked up by the FBI and who had previously urged that communism was the best hope of China, was not only reinstated in the State Department but promoted. And finally, under Acheson, placed in charge of all placements and promotions. . . .

This, ladies and gentlemen, gives you somewhat of a picture of the type of individuals

54

who have been helping to shape our foreign policy. In my opinion the State Department, which is one of the most important government departments, is thoroughly infested with Communists.

I have in my hand 57 cases of individuals who would appear to be either card carrying members or certainly loyal to the Communist Party, but who nevertheless are still helping to shape our foreign policy.

One thing to remember in discussing the communists in our Government is that we are not dealing with spies who get 30 pieces of silver to steal the blueprints of a new weapon. We are dealing with a far more sinister type of activity because it permits the enemy to guide and shape our policy. . . .

Source: U.S. Congress, Senate, *Congressional Record*, 81st Congress, 2nd sess., 1950.

THE SINO-SOVIET ALLIANCE: ZHOU ENLAI SPEECH OF FEBRUARY 14, 1950

The new Treaty of Friendship, Alliance and Mutual Assistance, the Agreement on the Chinese Changchum South-Manchurian railway, Port Arthur and Dairen, and the Agreement on granting credit to China have been signed today between the People's Republic of China and the Union of Soviet Socialist Republics and notes have been exchanged. The conclusion of the above treaty and agreements is based on the vital interests of the great peoples of China and the Soviet Union and indicates fraternal friendship and eternal co-operation between China and the Soviet Union. The conclusion of the treaty and agreements is a special expression of fervent assistance to the revolutionary cause of the Chinese people on the part of the Soviet Union directed by the policy of Generalissimo Stalin.

The great friendship between our two powers has been built up since the October Socialist Revolution. However, imperialism and the counter-revolutionary government of China hampered further co-operation between us. The victory of the Chinese people has brought about radical changes in the situation. The Chinese people, under the leadership of Chairman Mao Tse-tung, have set up the People's Republic of China and have formed a state having unprecedented unity and this has made sincere cooperation possible between our two great states. Thanks to the meetings and the exchange of opinions between Generalissimo Stalin and Chairman Mao Tse-tung, this possibility became a reality and the friendship, alliance and mutual assistance between China and the Soviet Union are sealed with the signed treaty. The imperialist bloc headed by American imperialism has resorted to all kinds of provocative methods attempting to frustrate the friendship between our two nations, but these ignominious attempts have utterly failed.

This treaty and these agreements will help the Chinese people to realize that they are not alone, and will help in the restoration and development of the Chinese economy. . . .

Permit me on behalf of the Chinese people to express gratitude to Generalissimo Stalin and the Soviet Government for this great friendship. . . .

Long live permanent friendship and eternal co-operation between China and the Soviet Union!

Source: People's China, March 1, 1950, pp. 28–29.

NSC-68
April 14, 1950

Two complex sets of factors have now basically altered this historical distribution of power. First the defeat of Germany and Japan and the decline of the British and French Empires have interacted with the development of the United States and the Soviet Union in such a way that power has increasingly gravitated to these two centers. Second, the Soviet Union, unlike previous aspirants to hegemony, is animated by a new fanatic faith, antithetical to our own, and seeks to impose its absolute authority over the rest of the world. Conflict has, therefore, become endemic and is waged, on the part of the Soviet Union, by violent or non-violent methods in accordance with the dictates of expediency.

The issues that face us are momentous, involving the fulfillment or destruction not only of this Republic but of civilization itself. They are issues which will not await our deliberations.

FUNDAMENTAL DESIGN OF THE KREMLIN

The fundamental design of those who control the Soviet Union and the international communist movement is to retain and solidify their absolute power, first in the Soviet Union and second in the areas now under their control. In the mind of the Soviet leaders, however, achievement of this design requires the dynamic extension of their authority and the ultimate elimination of any effective opposition to their authority.

The design, therefore, calls for the complete subversion or forcible destruction of the machinery of government and structure of society in the countries of the non-Soviet world and their replacement by an apparatus and structure subservient to and controlled from the Kremlin. To that end Soviet efforts are now directed toward the domination of the Eurasian land mass. The United States, as the principal center of power in the non-Soviet world and the bulwark of opposition to Soviet expansion, is the principal enemy whose integrity and vitality must be subverted or destroyed by one means or another if the Kremlin is to achieve its fundamental design.

THE UNDERLYING CONFLICT IN THE REALM OF IDEAS AND VALUES BETWEEN THE U.S. PURPOSE AND THE KREMLIN DESIGN

A. *Nature of Conflict*

The Kremlin regards the United States as the only major threat to the achievement of its fundamental design. There is a basic conflict between the idea of freedom under a government of laws, and the idea of slavery under the grim oligarchy of the Kremlin.

The assault on free institutions is world-wide now, and in the context of the present polarization of power a defeat of free institutions anywhere is a defeat everywhere.

Thus unwillingly our free society finds itself mortally challenged by the Soviet system.

No other value system is so wholly irreconcilable with ours, so implacable in its purpose to destroy ours, so capable of turning to its own uses the most dangerous and divisive trends in our own society, no other so skillfully and powerfully evokes the elements of irrationality in human nature everywhere, and no other has the support of a great and growing center of military power.

In a shrinking world, which now faces the threat of atomic warfare, it is not an adequate objective merely to seek to check the Kremlin design, for the absence of order among nations is becoming less and less tolerable. This fact imposes on us, in our own interests, the responsibility of world leadership. It demands that we make the attempt, and accept the risks inherent in it, to bring about order and justice by means consistent with the principles of freedom and democracy.

By practically demonstrating the integrity and validity of our system, the free world widens the area of possible agreement and thus can hope gradually to bring about a Soviet acknowledgement of realities which in sum will eventually constitute a frustration of the Soviet design. Short of this, however, it might be possible to create a situation which will induce the Soviet Union to accommodate itself, with or without the conscious abandonment of its design, to coexistence on tolerable terms with the non-Soviet world. Such a development would be a triumph for the idea of freedom and democracy. It must be an immediate objective of the United States.

The Kremlin's design for world domination begins at home. The first concern of a despotic oligarchy is that the local base of its power and authority be secure. The massive fact of the iron curtain isolating the Soviet peoples from the outside world, the repeated political purges within the USSR, and the institutionalized crimes of the [Soviet regime] are evidence that the Kremlin does not feel secure at home.

Being a totalitarian dictatorship, the Kremlin's objectives in these policies is the total subjective submission of the peoples now under its control. The concentration camp is the prototype of the society which these policies are designed to achieve.

Our overall policy at the present time may be described as one designed to foster a world environment in which the American system can survive and flourish. It therefore rejects the concept of isolation and affirms the necessity of our positive participation in the world community.

As for the policy of "containment," it is one which seeks by all means short of war to 1) block further expansion of Soviet power, 2) expose the falsities of Soviet pretensions, 3) induce a retraction of the Kremlin's control and influence and 4) in general, so foster the seeds of destruction within the Soviet system that the Kremlin is brought at least to the point of modifying its behavior to conform to generally accepted international standards.

It is quite clear from Soviet theory and practice that the Kremlin seeks to bring the free world under its dominion by the methods of the Cold War. Every institution of our society is an instrument which it is sought to stultify and turn against our purposes. Those that touch most closely our material and moral strength are obviously prime targets: labor unions, civic enterprises, schools, churches and all media for influencing opinion. The effort is not so much to make them serve obvious Soviet ends as to prevent them from serving our ends, and thus to make them sources of confusion in our economy, our culture, and our body politic.

Since everything that gives us or others respect for our institutions is a suitable object for attack, it also fits the Kremlin's design that where with impunity we can be insulted and made to suffer indignity the opportunity shall not be missed, particularly in any context which can be used to cast dishonor on our country, our system, our motives, or our methods.

Atomic Armaments

The United States now has an atomic capability, including both numbers and deliverability, estimated to be adequate, if effectively utilized, to deliver a serious blow against the war-making capacity of the USSR.

It is estimated that, within the next four years, the USSR will attain the capability of seriously damaging vital centers of the United States, provided it strikes a surprise blow and provided further that the blow is opposed by no more effective opposition than we now have programmed. Such a blow could so seriously damage the United States as to greatly reduce its superiority in economic potential

For the moment our atomic retaliatory capability is probably adequate to deter the Kremlin from a deliberate direct military attack against ourselves or other free peoples. However, when it calculates that it has a sufficient atomic capability to make a surprise attack on us, nullifying our atomic superiority and creating a military situation decisively in its favor, the Kremlin might be tempted to strike swiftly and with stealth. The existence of two large atomic capabilities in such a relationship might well act, therefore, not as a deterrent, but as an incitement to war.

In the event the USSR develops by 1954 the atomic capability which we now anticipate, it is hardly conceivable that, if war comes, the Soviet leaders would refrain from the use of atomic weapons unless they felt fully confident of attaining their objectives by other means.

Possible Courses of Action

Introduction. Four possible courses of action by the United States in the present situation can be distinguished. They are:

a. Continuation of current policies, with current and currently projected programs for carrying out these policies;
b. Isolation;
c. War; and
d. A more rapid building up of the political, economic, and military strength of the free world than that provided under (a) with the purpose of reaching, if possible, a tolerable state of order among nations without war and of preparing to defend ourselves in the event that the free world is attacked.

The role of negotiation. Negotiation must be considered in relation to these courses of action. The Soviet Union possesses several advantages over the free world in negotiations on any issue:

a. It can and does enforce secrecy on all significant facts about conditions within the Soviet Union;
b. It does not have to be responsive in any important sense to public opinion;
c. It does not have to consult and agree with any other countries on the terms it will offer and accept; and

d. It can influence public opinion in other countries while insulting the peoples under its control.

These are important advantages. Together with the unfavorable trend of our power position, they militate against successful negotiation of a general settlement at this time.

The problem is to create such political and economic conditions in the free world, backed by force sufficient to inhibit Soviet attack, that the Kremlin will accommodate itself to these conditions, gradually withdraw, and eventually change its policies drastically.

Clearly under present circumstances we will not be able to negotiate a settlement which calls for a change in the Soviet system. What then, is the role of negotiation?

The free countries must always be prepared to negotiate and must be ready to take the initiative at times in seeking negotiation. They must develop a negotiating position which defines the issues and the terms on which they would be prepared—and at what stages—to accept agreements with the Soviet Union.

A sound negotiating position is, therefore, an essential element in the ideological conflict. For some time after a decision to build up strength, any offer of, or attempt at, negotiating of a general settlement could be only a tactic.

In conclusion, negotiation is not a possible separate course of action but rather a means of gaining support for a program of building strength, of recording, where necessary and desirable, progress in the Cold War, and of facilitating further progress while helping to minimize the risks of war.

The United States is currently devoting about 22 percent of its gross national product (225 billion in 1949) to military expenditures (6 percent), foreign assistance (2 percent) and investment (14 percent), little of which is in war-supporting industries. In an emergency, the United States could devote upward of 50 percent of its gross national product to these purposes.

From the point of view of the economy as a whole, the program might not result in a real decrease in the standard of living, for the economic effects of the program might be to increase the gross national product by more than the amount being absorbed for additional military and foreign assistance purposes.

The threat to the free world involved in the development of the Soviet Union's atomic and other capabilities will rise steadily and rather rapidly. For the time being, the United States possesses a marked atomic superiority over the Soviet Union which, together with the potential capabilities of the United States and other free countries in other forces and weapons, inhibits aggressive Soviet action. This provides an opportunity for the United States, in cooperation with other free countries, to launch a build-up of strength which will support a firm policy directed to the frustration of the Kremlin design. The immediate goals of our efforts to build a successfully functioning political and economic system in the free world backed by adequate military strength is to postpone and avert the disastrous situation which, in light of the Soviet Union's probable fission bomb capability and possible thermo-nuclear bomb capability, might arise in 1954 on a continuation of our present programs. . . .

Source: Naval War College Review, XXVII, No. 6, Sequence No. 255 (May/June 1975), pp. 51–108.

U.N. RESOLUTION ON KOREA
June 27, 1950

Resolution concerning the complaint of aggression upon the Republic of Korea, adopted at the four hundred seventy-fourth meeting of the Security Council, on June 27, 1950:

The Security Council,

Having determined that the armed attack upon the Republic of Korea by forces from North Korea constitutes a breach of the peace, and

Having called for an immediate cessation of hostilities, and

Having called upon the authorities of North Korea to withdraw their armed forces to the 38th parallel, and

Having noted from the report of the United Nations Commission for Korea that the authorities in North Korea have neither ceased hostilities nor withdrawn their armed forces to the 38th parallel and that urgent military measures are required to restore international peace and security, and

Having noted the appeal of the Republic of Korea to the United Nations for immediate and effective steps to secure peace and security,

Recommends that the Members of the United Nations furnish such assistance to the Republic of Korea as may be necessary to repel the armed attack and to restore international peace and security in the area.

[*Voting for the resolution:* United States, United Kingdom, France, China, Norway, Ecuador and Cuba. *Voting against:* Yugoslavia. *Abstention:* Egypt, India (2 days later India accepted the resolution). *Absent:* Soviet Union.]

Source: Senate Foreign Relations and Armed Services Committees, *Hearings, Military Situation in the Far East,* Eighty-Second Congress, 1st session, Washington, D.C., 1950, p. 3369.

PRESIDENT HARRY TRUMAN'S STATEMENT ON THE KOREAN WAR
June 27, 1950

In Korea the government forces, which were armed to prevent border raids and to preserve internal security, were attacked by invading forces from North Korea. The Security Council of the United Nations called upon the invading troops to cease hostilities and to withdraw to the 38th Parallel. This they have not done, but on the contrary have pressed the attack. The Security Council called upon all members of the United Nations to render every assistance to the United Nations in the execution of this resolution. In these circumstances I have ordered United States air and sea forces to give the Korean government troops cover and support.

The attack upon Korea makes it plain beyond all doubt that communism has passed beyond the use of subversion to conquer independent nations and will now use armed invasion and war. It has defied the orders of the Security Council of the United Nations issued to preserve peace and security.

In these circumstances the occupation of Formosa by Communist forces would be a direct threat to the security of the Pacific area and to the United States forces performing their lawful and necessary functions in that area. Accordingly, I have ordered the Seventh Fleet to prevent any attack on Formosa. As a corollary of this action I am calling upon the Chinese Government on Formosa to cease all air and sea operations against the mainland. The Seventh Fleet will see that this is done.

I have similarly directed acceleration in the furnishing of military assistance to the forces of France and the associated states in Indochina and the dispatch of a military mission to provide close working relations with those forces.

Source: U.S. Department of State, *Bulletin,* July 3, 1950, vol. 23, Washington, D.C., p. 5.

SECRET SOVIET FOREIGN MINISTRY DOCUMENT ON THE KOREAN WAR AND ITS ARMISTICE
1966

Prepared for internal distribution.

I.

After separate elections in 1948 in South Korea and the formation of the puppet government of Syngman Rhee, on the one hand, and the formation of the DPRK, on the other, relations between the North and the South of the country were sharply aggravated. The Seoul regime, as well as the DPRK, declared its claim to be the authority in all of Korea. The situation at the 38th parallel became even more intense in 1948 after the withdrawal of Soviet and American troops from Korea.

During this period, Kim Il Sung and other Korean leaders were firmly determined to unify the country by military means, without devoting the necessary attention to studying the possibility that existed at that time for peaceful reunification through the broad development of the democratic movement in South Korea.

In the DPRK, a people's army was created which in manpower and equipment significantly surpassed the armed forces of South Korea. . . .

Calculating that the USA would not enter a war over South Korea, Kim Il Sung persistently pressed for agreement from Stalin and Mao Zedong to reunify the country by military means.

Stalin at first treated the persistent appeals of Kim Il Sung with reserve, noting that "such a large affair in relation to South Korea . . . needs much preparation," but he did not object in principle. The final agreement to support the plans of the Koreans was given by Stalin at the time of Kim Il Sung's visit to Moscow in March-April 1950. Following this, in May, Kim Il Sung visited Beijing and secured the support of Mao.

The Korean government envisioned realizing its goal in three stages:

1) concentration of troops near the 38th parallel
2) issuing an appeal to the South for peaceful unification
3) initiating military activity after the South's rejection of the proposal for peaceful unification.

At Stalin's order, all requests of the North Koreans for delivery of arms and equipment for the formation of additional units of the KPA (Korean People's Army) were quickly met. The Chinese leadership sent to Korea a division formed from Koreans who had been serving in the Chinese army, and promised to send food aid and to transfer one army closer to Korea "in case the Japanese enter on the side of South Korea.". . . .

At the insistence of Kim Il Sung, the beginning of military activity was scheduled for June 25th, 1950.

By the time of the attack, the North Korean armed forces had significant superiority over the South Koreans. . . . The operational plan of the KPA envisioned that Korean troops . . . would in the main complete military activity within 22–27 days.

II.

During Kim Il Sung's visit to Beijing in May 1950, Mao Zedong, in conversation with him, underscored his conviction that the Americans would not become engaged in a war "for such a small territory as Korea.". . .

In August 1950 American planes began bombing Chinese territory near the Yalu. In October 1950, soon after the American landing at Inchon, the front line moved close to the Korean-Chinese border and the enemy's artillery began to fire on Chinese territory. Ships of the American Seventh Fleet entered the Taiwan Straits.

By that time the Korean People's Army had virtually disintegrated as a fighting force. . . .

The Chinese government, under pressure from Stalin, adopted the decision to send volunteers to Korea only after a real threat to the security of China had arisen and the very existence of the DPRK had been called into question. The entry of Chinese volunteers into Korea began in the second half of October 1950. Subsequently, the total number of Chinese troops in Korea was brought to 1 million men. . . .

The entry of the Chinese volunteers into the war and the active participation of Soviet military advisers, who participated in the planning of all major offensive operations, brought about a vital breakthrough in the course of military events. . . .

During this period of the war, sharp disagreements arose between Kim Il Sung and the command of the Chinese People's volunteers, led by Peng Dehuai. The Koreans were against the surrender of Seoul by the Chinese volunteers and reproached them for not supporting the Korean units on the eastern front. . . .

IV. NEGOTIATIONS FOR THE ARMISTICE

By the middle of 1951, the situation clearly indicated that it was in practice impossible to resolve the unification of Korea by military means. . . . After consultations with the Chinese and Koreans, the Soviet government on June 23, 1951, put forward a proposal for settling the military conflict. . . .

The negotiations of the representatives of the commands of the warring sides began on July 10, 1951, and continued, with breaks, for more than two years, until the end of July 1953. . . .

By the beginning of May 1952, an agreement was reached on all questions, with the exception of the question regarding prisoners of war. . . .

Measures undertaken by the Soviet government after the death of Stalin in many ways facilitated the conclusion of the agreement. While in Moscow for Stalin's funeral, Zhou Enlai had conversations with Soviet leaders regarding the situation in Korea. During these conversations, Zhou Enlai, in the name of the government of the PRC, urgently proposed that the Soviet side assist the speeding up of the negotiations and the conclusion of an armistice. Such a position by the Chinese coincided with our position. For the implementation of practical measures ensuing from the complicated situation, a special representative was sent to Pyongyang from Moscow in March 1953 with a proposal for speeding up the peace negotiations. By that time Koreans also showed a clear aspiration for the most rapid cessation of military activity.

On July 27th an armistice agreement was signed. . . .

Source: Cold War International History Project, *Bulletin: From the Russian Archives,* Woodrow Wilson International Center for Scholars, Washington, D.C., Fall 1993, Issue 3, pp. 15–18.

PRESIDENT TRUMAN'S RADIO ADDRESS EXPLAINING GENERAL MacARTHUR'S DISMISSAL
April 11, 1951

I want to talk plainly to you tonight about what we are doing in Korea and about our policy in the Far East. In the simplest terms, what we are doing in Korea is this:

We are trying to prevent a third world war.

It is right for us to be in Korea. It was right last June. It is right today.

I want to remind you why this is true.

The Communists in the Kremlin are engaged in a monstrous conspiracy to stamp out freedom all over the world. If they were to succeed, the United States would be numbered among their principal victims. In must be clear to everyone that the United States cannot—and will not—sit idly by and await foreign conquest. The only question is: When is the best time to meet the threat and how is the best way to meet it?

The best time to meet the threat is in the beginning. It is easier to put out a fire in the beginning when it is small than after it has become a roaring blaze.

And the best way to meet the threat of aggression is for the peace-loving nations to act together, to crush the aggression of the dictators, and if they had acted in the beginning, when the aggression was small, there probably would have been no World War II.

If history has taught us anything, it is that aggression anywhere in the world is a threat to peace everywhere in the world. When that aggression is supported by the cruel and selfish rulers of a powerful nation who are bent on conquest, it becomes a clear and present danger to the security and independence of every nation.

This is a lesson that most people in this country have learned thoroughly. This is the basic reason why we joined in creating the United Nations. And, since the end of World War II, we have been putting that lesson into practice—we have been working with other free nations to check the aggressive designs of the Soviet Union before they can result in a third world war.

That is what we did in Greece, when that nation was threatened by the aggression of international communism.

Another big Communist threat to peace was the Berlin blockade. That too could have led to war. But again it was settled because free men would not back down in an emergency.

The aggression against Korea was part of a greater plan for conquering all of Asia.

I have a secret intelligence report here. This one tells what another Communist officer in the Far East told his men several months before the invasion of Korea. Here is what he said: "In order to successfully undertake the long awaited world revolution, we must first unify Asia. Java, Indo-China, Malaysia, India, Tibet, Thailand, the Philippines and Japan are our ultimate targets. The United States is the only obstacle on our rise for the liberation of all countries in southeast Asia. In other words, we must unify the people of Asia and crush the United States."

That is what the Communist leaders are telling their people, and that is what they have been trying to do.

Again, "liberation" in Commie language means "conquest."

They want to control all Asia from the Kremlin.

This plan of conquest is in flat contradiction to what we believe. We believe that all the nations of Asia should be free to work out their affairs in their own way. This is the basis of peace in the Far East and it is the basis of peace everywhere else.

The question we have had to face is whether the Communist plan of conquest can be stopped without general war. Our Government and other countries associated with us in the United Nations believe that the best chance of stopping it without general war is to meet the attack in Korea and defeat it there.

So far, by fighting a limited war in Korea, we have prevented aggression from succeeding and bringing on general war. And the ability of the whole free world to resist Communist aggression has been greatly improved.

Our resolute stand in Korea is helping the forces of freedom now fighting in Indochina and other countries in that part of the world. It has already slowed down the timetable of conquest.

We do not want to see the conflict in Korea extended. We are trying to prevent a world war—not to start one.

But you may ask why can't we take other steps to punish the aggressor. Why don't we bomb Manchuria and China itself? Why don't we assist Chinese Nationalist troops to land on the mainland of China?

If we were to do these things [we] would be running a very grave risk of starting a general war. If that were to happen, we would have brought about the exact situation we are trying to prevent.

The dangers are great. Make no mistake about it. Behind the North Koreans and Chinese stand the tanks, the planes, the submarines, the soldiers, and the scheming rulers of the Soviet Union.

Our aim is to avoid the spread of the conflict.

If the Communist authorities realize that they cannot defeat us in Korea, if they realize it would be foolhardy to widen the hostilities beyond Korea, then they may recognize the folly of continuing their aggression. A peaceful settlement may then be possible. The door is always open.

A number of events have made it evident that General MacArthur did not agree with that policy. I have, therefore, considered it essential to relieve General MacArthur so that there would be no doubt or confusion as to the real purpose and aim of our policy.

It was with the deepest personal regret that I found myself compelled to take this action. General MacArthur is one of our greatest military commanders. But the cause of world peace is more important than any individual.

We are ready, at any time, to negotiate for a restoration of peace in the area. But we will not engage in appeasement. We are only interested in real peace.

A settlement founded upon these elements would open the way for unification of Korea and the withdrawal of all foreign forces.

Source: Senate Foreign Relations and Armed Services Committees, *Hearings, Military Situation in the Far East,* Eighty-second Congress, First session, 1951, pp. 3547–51.

GENERAL DOUGLAS MacARTHUR'S
ADDRESS TO CONGRESS
April 19, 1951

I do not stand here as advocate for any partisan cause, for the issues are fundamental and reach quite beyond the realm of partisan consideration. They must be resolved on the highest plane of national interest if our course is to prove sound and our future protected.

The Communist threat is a global one. Its successful advance in one sector threatens the destruction of every other sector. You cannot appease or otherwise surrender to communism in Asia without simultaneously undermining our efforts to halt its advance in Europe. . . .

With this brief insight into the surrounding areas I now turn to the Korean conflict. Our victory was complete and our objectives within reach when Red China intervened with numerically superior ground forces. This created a new war and an entirely new situation, a situation which called for new decisions in the diplomatic sphere to permit the realistic adjustment of military strategy. Such decisions have not been forthcoming.

While no man in his right mind would advocate sending our ground forces into continental China—and such was never given a thought—the new situation did urgently demand a drastic revision of strategic planning.

I felt that military necessity in the conduct of war made necessary:

> First, the intensification of our economic blockade against China.
> Second, the imposition of a naval blockade against the China coast.
> Third, removal of restrictions on air reconnaissance of China's coastal areas and of Manchuria.
> Fourth, removal of restrictions on the forces of the Republic of China on Formosa.

I called for reinforcements, but was informed that reinforcements were not available. I made clear that if not permitted to utilize the friendly Chinese force of some 600,000 men on Formosa; if not permitted to blockade the China coast to prevent the Chinese Reds from getting succor from without; and if there were to be no hope of major reinforcements, the position of the command from the military standpoint forbade victory. I have constantly called for the new political decisions essential to a solution. Efforts have been made to distort my position. It has been said in effect that I was a warmonger. Nothing could be further from the truth.

But once war is forced upon us, there is no other alternative than to apply every available means to bring it to a swift end. War's very objective is victory—not prolonged indecision. In war, indeed, there can be no substitute for victory.

There are some who for varying reasons would appease Red China. They are blind to history's clear lesson. For history teaches with unmistakable emphasis that appeasement but begets new and bloodier war. It points to no single instance where the end has justified the means—where appeasement has led to more than a sham peace.

I am closing my 52 years of military service. When I joined the Army even before the turn of the century, it was the fulfillment of all my boyish hopes and dreams. The world has turned over many times since I took an oath on the plains at West Point, and the hopes and dreams have long since vanished. But I still remember the refrain of one of the most popular barrack ballads of that day which proclaimed most proudly that—

"Old soldiers never die; they just fade away."

And like the old soldier of that ballad, I now close my military career and just fade away—an old soldier who tried to do his duty as God gave him the light to see that duty.

Good-by.

Source: U.S. Congress, Senate, Joint Committee on Armed Services and Foreign Relations, *Military Situation in the Far East,* 82nd Congress, First Session, Washington, D.C., Government Printing Office, 1951, pp. 3553–58.

McCARTHY ATTACKS GENERAL MARSHALL AND SECRETARY OF STATE ACHESON
July 14, 1951

Mr. President, in closely following the testimony before the Joint Committee on Foreign Relations and Armed Services, sitting jointly, which is conducting an investigation of the dismissal of Douglas MacArthur, I have become more and more impressed by two inescapable facts:

First. That it is impossible to develop the facts in the MacArthur inquiry without at the same time bringing to light some of the facts which bear on the question of why we fell from our position as the most powerful Nation on earth at the end of World War II to a position of declared weakness by our leadership.

Second. That it will be equally impossible to obtain the answers to the above without uncovering a conspiracy so immense and an infamy so black as to dwarf any previous such venture in the history of man. During the Marshall testimony, one of the Senators, obviously troubled by the odor of the conspiracy which was commencing to rise as a result of the constant probing by the members of the committee—troubled by the fringes of the conspiracy which were commencing to show—came to my office and asked me for information on a subject which was troubling and puzzling him greatly. While I cannot quote him verbatim, the questions he asked were substantially as follows:

First. Who was close to Marshall and succeeded in deceiving this great American at Yalta when his military advice was that we turn Manchuria over to Russia, thereby signing at least the first section in the death warrant of the Republic of China?

Second. Who twisted and perverted the thinking of this great American and misguided him into the folly of his disastrous mission to China?

Third. Who, of tortured disloyalty to America, succeeded in deceiving this great general during the course of World War II to the end that he always sided with Stalin and against Churchill when history's great decisions were being made—decisions which turned out so bad for the free world and so good for international communism?

Upon searching for the answers for the Senator, I found to my surprise that Marshall, who, by the alchemy of propaganda, became the "greatest living American," and the recently proclaimed "master of global strategy" for the party in power, has never had his record subjected to the searching light of any historian. In view of the fact that the committee, the Congress, and the American people are being called upon either to endorse or reject Marshall's global strategy, I felt that it was urgent that such a study be made and submitted to the Russell committee. . . .

It is needless to tell you that this was a monumental task, but one which I felt had to be done, for unless we understand the record of Marshall it will be impossible to even remotely grasp the planned steady retreat from victory which commenced long before World War II ended. Unless we carefully study the records of Marshall and Acheson, who have worked together so closely, it will be impossible to foretell the next move on the timetable of the great conspiracy.

This administration, which has given us this caricature of a war, is now bent on an even worse horror—a phony and fraudulent peace. It is planned by Secretary Marshall and the elegant and alien Acheson—Russian as to heart, British as to manner. We even hear cries for a fraudulent peace within this Chamber. In support of their campaign for a fraudulent peace, its advocates wage a campaign of fear. . . .

I do not think we need fear too much about the Communists dropping atomic bombs on Washington. They would kill too many of their friends that way. . . .

We have observed what calamities might have befallen the allied cause had Roosevelt accepted Marshall's persistent demand for a "second front now." We have seen the equivocal and dangerous nature of his counsel with reference to the North African invasion. We have observed how closely he fitted his views into those of Stalin over every major issue of the war. We have seen further how in his instructions to General Deane, his refusal to exercise foresight over the corridor to Berlin, and his wish that the Russians might first enter that great and shattered city, General Marshall's decisions paralleled the interests of the Kremlin. . . .

I do not at this time discuss the question of whether General Marshall was aware that he was implementing the will of Stalin in these matters. I do not propose to go into his motives. Unless one has all the tangled and often complicated circumstances contributing to a man's decisions, an inquiry into his motives is often fruitless. I do not pretend to understand General Marshall's nature and character, and I shall leave that subject to subtler analysts of human personality. . . .

It was Marshall who stood at Roosevelt's elbow at Yalta, urging the grim necessity of bribing Stalin to get into the war. It was Marshall who submitted intelligence reports to support his argument, suppressing more truthful estimates, as we are informed in Hanson Baldwin's book on page 81, and keeping from the stricken Roosevelt knowledge that the Japanese were even then feeling for peace in acknowledgement to defeat. . . .

It was Marshall who selected the line for the division of Korea which was chosen by the Russian Foreign Office and General Staff nearly 50 years ago. We restored their pre-1904 claims on North Korea at the Pentagon in August of 1945. . . .

I think it is now transparently clear why Marshall went to China. Having, with the Yalta crowd, framed the China policy, he was intent on executing it down to its last dreadful clause and syllable and it is, I think, significant that he tarried in China for 13 arduous months, and when he left it was obvious to all beholders that China must fall to the Russian Empire. . . .

The Forrestal plan would have strengthened us in the conflict with Russia. The result of using the Marshall plan instead of the Forrestal plan in Europe has been to make us the patsy of the modern world, to arouse the contempt and suspicion of Europe and to leave us, in the summer of 1951, heavily engaged in Asia, and with no willing, reliable allies in all Europe among the beneficiaries of our bounty except Greece and Turkey and, a country that had no seat at the table at all, Spain, plus Western Germany whose resources we cannot use in the struggle against international communism because her 48,000,000 people according to the State Department are not peace-loving. . . .

I do not think that this monstrous perversion of sound and understandable national policy was accidental. I think it was an evil hoax on the generosity, good will and carelessness of the American people. I think that it was the product of a will and intention hostile to this free society. . . .

Of all Marshall's significant endeavors since the early months of World War II, the derricking of the Forrestal plan ranks next, I should judge, to the Marshall policy for China in its massive helpfulness to the world ambitions of the Kremlin. That judgment is in no way impaired by the fact that Russia declined and forbade its satellites to share in the Marshall plan's bounty. . . .

How can we account for our present situation unless we believe that men high in this Government are concerting to deliver us to disaster? This must be the product of a great conspiracy, a conspiracy on a scale so immense as to dwarf any previous such venture in the history of man. A conspiracy of infamy so black that, when it is finally exposed, its principals shall be forever deserving of the maledictions of all honest men.

Who constitutes the highest circles of this conspiracy? About that we cannot be sure. We are convinced that Dean Acheson, who steadfastly serves the interests of nations other than his own, the friend of Alger Hiss, who supported him in his hour of retribution, who contributed to his defense fund, must be high on the roster. The President? He is their captive. I have wondered, as have you, why he did not dispense with so great a liability as Acheson to his own and his party's interest. It is now clear to me. In the relationship of master and man, did you ever hear of man firing master? Truman is a satisfactory front. He is only dimly aware of what is going on. . . .

What can be made of this unbroken series of decisions and acts contributing to the strategy of defeat? They cannot be attributed to incompetence. If Marshall were merely stupid, the laws of probability would dictate that part of his decisions would serve this country's interest. If Marshall is innocent of guilty intention, how could he be trusted to guide the defense of this country further? We have declined so precipitously in relation to the Soviet Union in the last 6 years. How much swifter may be our fall into disaster with Marshall at the helm? Where will all this stop? That is not a rhetorical question: Ours is not a rhetorical danger. Where next will Marshall carry us? It is useless to suppose that his nominal superior will ask him to resign. He cannot even dispense with Acheson.

What is the objective of the great conspiracy? I think it is clear from what has occurred and is now occurring: to diminish the United States in world affairs, to weaken us militarily, to confuse our spirit with talk of surrender in the Far East and to impair our will to resist evil. To what end? To the end that we shall be contained, frustrated and finally fall victim to Soviet intrigue from within and Russian military might from without. Is that farfetched? There have been many examples in history of rich and powerful states which have been corrupted from within, enfeebled and deceived until they were unable to resist aggression. . . .

It is the great crime of the Truman administration that it has refused to undertake the job of ferreting the enemy from its ranks. I once puzzled over that refusal. The President, I said, is a loyal American; why does he not lead in this enterprise? I think that I know why he does not. The President is not master in his own house. Those who are master there not only have a desire to protect the sappers and miners—they could not do otherwise. They themselves are not free. They belong to a larger conspiracy, the world-wide web of which has been spun from Moscow. It was Moscow, for example, which decreed that the United States should execute its loyal friend, the Republic of China. The executioners were that well-identified group headed by Acheson and George Catlett Marshall.

Source: U.S. Congress, Senate, *Congressional Record*, 82nd Congress, 1st Session, 1951, pp. 97, 6556, 6557, 6566, 6570, 6572, 6573, 6581, 6593, 6594, 6601, 6602, 6603.

VI

THE EISENHOWER ADMINISTRATION

D O C U M E N T   1

J.F. DULLES ON "MASSIVE RETALIATION"
January 12, 1954

... The Soviet Communists are planning for what they call "an entire historical era," and we should do the same. They seek, through many types of maneuvers, gradually to divide and weaken the free nations by overextending them in efforts which, as Lenin put it, are "beyond their strength, so that they come to practical bankruptcy." Then, said Lenin, "our victory is assured." Then, said Stalin, will be "the moment for the decisive blow."

In the face of this strategy, measures cannot be judged adequate merely because they ward off an immediate danger. It is essential to do this, but it is also essential to do so without exhausting ourselves.

When the Eisenhower administration applied this test, we felt that some transformations were needed. It is not sound military strategy permanently to commit U.S. land forces to Asia to a degree that leaves us no strategic reserves. It is not sound economics, or good foreign policy, to support permanently other countries; for in the long run, that creates as much ill will as good will. Also, it is not sound to become permanently committed to military expenditures so vast they lead to "practical bankruptcy". . . .

The Eisenhower administration seeks, ... for ourselves and the other free nations, a maximum deterrent at a bearable cost.

Local defense will always be important. But there is no local defense which alone will contain the mighty land power of the Communist world. Local defenses must be reinforced by the further deterrent of massive retaliatory power. A potential aggressor must know that he cannot always prescribe battle conditions that suit him. Otherwise, for example, a potential aggressor, who is glutted with manpower, might be tempted to attack in confidence that resistance would be confined to manpower. He might be tempted to attack in places where his superiority was decisive.

The way to deter aggression is for the free community to be willing and able to respond vigorously at places and with means of its own choosing. . . .

The basic decision [of the President is] to depend primarily upon a great capacity to retaliate, instantly, by means and at places of our choosing. . . . That permits of a selection of military means instead of a multiplication of means. As a result, it is now possible to get, and share, more basic security at less cost.

Let us now see how this concept has been applied to foreign policy, taking first the Far East.

In Korea this administration effected a major transformation. The fighting has been stopped on honorable terms. That was possible because the aggressor, already thrown back to and behind his place of beginning, was faced with the possibility that the fighting might to his own great peril, soon spread beyond the limits and methods which he had selected. . . .

74

In the ways I outlined we gather strength for the long-term defense of freedom. . . . It is normal that at some times and at some places there may be setbacks to the cause of freedom ... [but] if we can deter such aggression as would mean general war, and that is our confident resolve, then we let can time and fundamentals work for us. . . .

Source: Department of State *Bulletin,* Vol. XXX, pp. 107-10.

CONGRESSIONAL RESOLUTION ON FORMOSA
January 29, 1955

[handwritten: Taiwan]

Whereas the primary purpose of the United States, in its relations with all other nations, is to develop and sustain a just and enduring peace for all; and

Whereas certain territories in the West Pacific under the jurisdiction of the Republic of China are now under armed attack, and threats and declarations have been and are being made by the Chinese Communists that such armed attack is in aid of and in preparation for armed attack on Formosa and the Pescadores; and

Whereas such armed attack if continued would gravely endanger the peace and security of the West Pacific Area and particularly of Formosa and the Pescadores; and

Whereas the secure possession by friendly governments of the Western Pacific Island chain, of which Formosa is a part, is essential to the vital interests of the United States and all friendly nations in or bordering upon the Pacific Ocean; and

Whereas the President of the United States on January 6, 1955, submitted to the Senate for its advice and consent to ratification a Mutual Defense Treaty between the United States of America and the Republic of China, which recognizes that an armed attack in the West Pacific area directed against territories, therein described, in the region of Formosa and the Pescadores, would be dangerous to the peace and safety of the parties to the treaty: Therefore be it

Resolved by the Senate and House of Representatives of the United States of America in Congress assembled, That the President of the United States be and he hereby is authorized to employ the Armed Forces of the United States as he deems necessary for the specific purpose of securing and protecting Formosa and the Pescadores against armed attack, this authority to include the security and protection of such related positions and territories of that area now in friendly hands and the taking of such other measures as he judges to be required or appropriate in assuring the defense of Formosa and the Pescadores.

This resolution shall expire when the President shall determine that the peace and security of the area is reasonably assured by international conditions created by action of the United Nations or otherwise, and shall so report to the Congress.

Source: Public Law, 84th Congress.

THE EISENHOWER DOCTRINE
March 9, 1957

. . .

Sec. 2. The President is authorized to undertake, in the general area of the Middle East, military assistance programs with any nation or group of nations of that area desiring such assistance. Furthermore, the United States regards as vital to the national interest and world peace the preservation of the independence and integrity of the nations of the Middle East. To this end, if the President determines the necessity thereof, the United States is prepared to use armed force to assist any such nation or group of nations requesting assistance against armed aggression from any country controlled by international communism. . . .

Source: The Eisenhower Doctrine, March 9, 1957, U.S. Department of State *Bulletin,* March 25, 1957, Vol. 36, p. 481.

PRESIDENT EISENHOWER ON THE U-2 INCIDENT
May 25, 1960

. . . Our safety, and that of the free world, demand, of course, effective systems for gathering information about the military capabilities of other powerful nations, especially those that make a fetish of secrecy. This involves many techniques and methods. In these times of vast military machines and nuclear-tipped missiles, the ferreting out of this information is indispensable to free-world security.

This has long been one of my most serious preoccupations. It is part of my grave responsibility, within the over-all problem of protecting the American people, to guard ourselves and our allies against surprise attack.

During the period leading up to World War II we learned from bitter experience the imperative necessity of a continuous gathering of intelligence information, the maintenance of military communications and contact, and alertness of command. . . .

Moreover, as President, charged by the Constitution with the conduct of America's foreign relations, and as Commander-in-Chief, charged with the direction of the operations and activities of our Armed Forces and their supporting services, I take full responsibility for approving all the various programs undertaken by our government to secure and evaluate military intelligence.

It was in the prosecution of one of these intelligence programs that the widely publicized U-2 incident occurred.

Aerial photography has been one of many methods we have used to keep ourselves and the free world abreast of major Soviet military developments. The usefulness of this work has been well established through four years of effort. The Soviets were well aware of it. Chairman Khrushchev has stated that he became aware of these flights several years ago. Only last week, in his Paris press conference, Chairman Khrushchev confirmed that he knew of these flights when he visited the United States last September. . . .

The plain truth is this: . . . there is no time when vigilance can be relaxed. Incidentally, from Pearl Harbor we learned that even negotiation itself can be used to conceal preparations for a surprise attack.

Next, as to our government's initial statement about the flight, this was issued to protect the pilot, his mission, and our intelligence processes, at a time when the true facts were still undetermined.

Our first information about the failure of this mission did not disclose whether the pilot was still alive, was trying to escape, was avoiding interrogation, or whether both plane and pilot had been destroyed. Protection of our intelligence system and the pilot, and concealment of the plane's mission, seemed imperative. It must be remembered that over a long period these flights had given us information of the greatest importance to the nation's security. In fact, their success has been nothing short of remarkable. . . .

I then made two facts clear to the public: first, our program of aerial reconnaissance had been undertaken with my approval; second, this government is compelled to keep abreast, by one means or another, of military activities of the Soviets, just as their government has for years engaged in espionage activities in our country and throughout the world. . . .

A major American goal is a world of open societies. . . . I offered five years ago to open our skies to Soviet reconnaissance aircraft on a reciprocal basis. The Soviets refused. That offer is still open. . . .

Source: Public Papers of the Presidents: Dwight D. Eisenhower, 1960, no. 163.

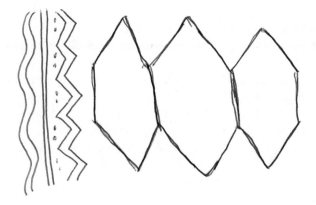

EISENHOWER'S FAREWELL ADDRESS
January 1961

. . .

We now stand ten years past the midpoint of a century that has witnessed four major wars among great nations. Three of them involved our own country. . . .

A vital element in keeping the peace is our military establishment. . . .

We annually spend on military security more than the net income of all United States corporations.

This conjunction of an immense military establishment and a large arms industry is new in the American experience. The total influence—economic, political, even spiritual—is felt in every city, every statehouse, every office of the federal government. We recognize the imperative need for this development. Yet we must not fail to comprehend its grave implications. Our toil, resources, and livelihood are all involved; so is the very structure of our society.

In the councils of government, we must guard against the acquisition of unwarranted influence, whether sought or unsought, by the military-industrial complex. The potential for the disastrous rise of misplaced power exists and will persist.

We must never let the weight of this combination endanger our liberties or democratic processes. . . .

Akin to, and largely responsible for, the sweeping changes in our industrial-military posture, has been the technological revolution during recent decades.

In this revolution, research has become central; it also becomes more formalized, complex and costly. A steadily increasing share is conducted for, by, or at the direction of, the federal government. . . .

The prospect of domination of the nation's scholars by federal employment, project allocations, and the power of money is ever-present—and is gravely to be regarded.

Yet, in holding scientific research and discovery in respect, as we should, we must also be alert to the equal and opposite dangers that public policy could itself become the captive of a scientific-technological elite. . . .

Source: *Public Papers of the Presidents: Dwight D. Eisenhower,* 1960-61, Government Printing Office, Washington, D.C., no. 421.

VII

THE KENNEDY AND JOHNSON ADMINISTRATIONS

PRESIDENT JOHN F. KENNEDY INAUGURAL ADDRESS
January 20, 1961

We observe today not a victory of party but a celebration of freedom—symbolizing an end as well as a beginning—signifying renewal as well as change. For I have sworn before you and Almighty God the same solemn oath our forebears prescribed nearly a century and three quarters ago.

The world is very different now. For man holds in his mortal hands the power to abolish all forms of human poverty and all forms of human life. And yet the same revolutionary beliefs for which our forebears fought are still at issue around the globe—the belief that the rights of man come not from the generosity of the state but from the hand of God.

We dare not forget today that we are the heirs of that first revolution. Let the word go forth from this time and place, to friend and foe alike, that the torch has been passed to a new generation of Americans—born in this century, tempered by war, disciplined by a hard and bitter peace, proud of our ancient heritage—and unwilling to witness or permit the slow undoing of those human rights to which this nation has always been committed. . . .

Let every nation know, whether it wishes us well or ill, that we shall pay any price, bear any burden, meet any hardship, support any friend, oppose any foe to assure the survival and the success of liberty. . . .

In the long history of the world, only a few generations have been granted the role of defending freedom in its hour of maximum danger. I do not shrink from this responsibility—I welcome it. I do not believe that any of us would exchange places with any other people or any other generation. The energy, the faith, the devotion which we bring to this endeavor will light our country and all who serve it—and the glow from that fire can truly light the world.

And so, my fellow Americans: ask not what your country can do for you—ask what you can do for your country.

My fellow citizens of the world: ask not what America will do for you, but what together we can do for the freedom of man. . . .

Source: Public Papers of the Presidents of the United States: John F. Kennedy, 1961. Washington, D.C., Government Printing Office, 1962, pp. 1–3.

PRESIDENT JOHN F. KENNEDY: ADDRESS TO THE AMERICAN PEOPLE ON THE SOVIET INSTALLATION OF MISSILES IN CUBA

October 22, 1962

This Government ... has maintained the closest surveillance of the Soviet military buildup on the island of Cuba. Within the past week, unmistakable evidence has established the fact that a series of offensive missile sites is now in preparation on that imprisoned island. The purpose of these bases can be none other than to provide a nuclear strike capability against the Western Hemisphere. . . .

The characteristics of these new missile sites indicate two distinct types of installations. Several of them include medium range ballistic missiles, capable of carrying a nuclear warhead for a distance of more than 1,000 nautical miles. Each of these missiles is capable of striking Washington, D.C., the Panama Canal, Cape Canaveral, Mexico City, or any other city in the southeastern part of the United States, in Central America, or in the Caribbean area.

Additional sites not yet completed appear to be designed for intermediate range ballistic missiles . . . capable of striking most of the major cities in the Western Hemisphere. . . .

This urgent transformation of Cuba into an important strategic base—by the presence of these large, long-range, and clearly offensive weapons of sudden mass destruction—constitutes an explicit threat to the peace and security of all the Americas. . . .

Neither the United States of America nor the world community of nations can tolerate deliberate deception and offensive threats on the part of any nation. . . .

Nuclear weapons are so destructive and ballistic missiles are so swift, that any substantially increased possibility of their use or any sudden change in their deployment may well be regarded as a definite threat to peace. . . .

Our own strategic missiles have never been transferred to the territory of any other nation under a cloak of secrecy and deception; . . . we have no desire to dominate or conquer any other nation or impose our system upon its people. . . .

This sudden, clandestine decision to station strategic weapons for the first time outside of Soviet soil—is a deliberately provocative and unjustified change in the status quo which cannot be accepted by this country. . . .

The 1930s taught us a clear lesson: aggressive conduct, if allowed to go unchecked and unchallenged, ultimately leads to war. . . .

I have directed that the following *initial* steps be taken immediately:

First: To halt this offensive buildup, a strict quarantine on all offensive military equipment under shipment to Cuba is being initiated. . . .

Second: . . . Should these offensive military preparations continue, thus increasing the threat to the hemisphere, further action will be justified. I have directed the Armed Forces to prepare for any eventualities; . . .

Third: It shall be the policy of this Nation to regard any nuclear missile launched from Cuba against any nation in the Western Hemisphere as an attack by the Soviet Union on the United States, requiring a full retaliatory response upon the Soviet Union. . . .

Seventh and finally: I call upon Chairman [Nikita] Khrushchev to halt and eliminate this clandestine, reckless, and provocative threat to world peace. . . . I call upon him further to abandon this course of world domination, and to join in an historic effort to end the perilous arms race. . . .

My fellow citizens: let no one doubt that this is a difficult and dangerous effort on which we have set out. No one can foresee precisely what course it will take or what costs or casualties will be incurred. . . . But the greatest danger of all would be to do nothing.

Source: Public Papers of the Presidents of the United States: John F. Kennedy, 1962. Washington, D.C., Government Printing Office, 1963.

PARTIAL TEST-BAN TREATY
July 25, 1963

TREATY

**Banning nuclear weapon tests in the
atmosphere, in outer space and under water**

The Governments of the United States of America, the United Kingdom of Great Britain and Northern Ireland, and the Union of Soviet Socialist Republics, hereinafter referred to as the "Original Parties",

Proclaiming as their principal aim the speediest possible achievement of an agreement on general and complete disarmament under strict international control, in accordance with the objectives of the United Nations, which would put an end to the armaments race and eliminate the incentive to the production and testing of all kinds of weapons, including nuclear weapons,

Seeking to achieve the discontinuance of all test explosions of nuclear weapons for all time, determined to continue negotiations to this end, and desiring to put an end to the contamination of man's environment by radioactive substances,

Have agreed as follows:

Article I

1. Each of the Parties to this Treaty undertakes to prohibit, to prevent, and not to carry out any nuclear weapon test explosion, or any other nuclear explosion, at any place under its jurisdiction or control:
   (a) in the atmosphere; beyond its limits, including outer space; or under water, including territorial waters or high seas; or
   (b) in any other environment if such explosion causes radioactive debris to be present outside the territorial limits of the State under whose jurisdiction or control such explosion is conducted. It is understood in this connection that the provisions of this subparagraph are without prejudice to the conclusion of a treaty resulting in the permanent banning of all nuclear test explosions, including all such explosions underground, the conclusion of which, as the Parties have stated in the Preamble to this Treaty, they seek to achieve.
2. Each of the Parties to this Treaty undertakes furthermore to refrain from causing, encouraging, or in any way participating in, the carrying out of any nuclear weapon test explosion, or any other nuclear explosion, anywhere which would take place in any of the environments described. . . .

Article IV

This Treaty shall be of unlimited duration.

Each Party shall in exercising its national sovereignty have the right to withdraw from the Treaty if it decides that extraordinary events, related to the subject matter of this Treaty, have jeopardized the supreme interests of its country. It shall give notice of such withdrawal to all other Parties to the Treaty three months in advance.

Source: U.S. Department of State, _Bulletin,_ 1963, Vol. 49, pp. 239–40.

THE TONKIN GULF RESOLUTION
August 7, 1964

That the Congress approves and supports the determination of the President, as Commander in Chief, to take all necessary measures to repel any armed attack against the forces of the United States and to prevent further aggression.*

*Resolution adopted by House of Representatives by vote of 416 to 0. U.S. Senate adopted resolution by vote of 88 to 2. Senators Morse of Oregon and Gruening of Alaska the two dissenters.

Source: U.S. Congress. 88th Congress, 2nd session, 1964. Congressional Record, Vol. 101, p. 18133.

STATE DEPARTMENT "WHITE PAPER" ON VIETNAM WAR
February 1965

INTRODUCTION

South Vietnam is fighting for its life against a brutal campaign of terror and attack inspired, directed, supplied, and controlled by the Communist regime in Hanoi. . . .

The war in Vietnam is a new kind of war, a fact as yet poorly understood in most parts of the world. Much of the confusion that prevails in the thinking of many people, and even many governments, stems from this basic misunderstanding. For in Vietnam a totally new brand of aggression has been loosed against an independent people who want to make their own way in peace and freedom. . . .

Above all, the war in Vietnam is *not* a spontaneous and local rebellion against the established government.

There are elements in the Communist program of conquest directed against South Vietnam common to each of the previous areas of aggression and subversion. But there is one fundamental difference. In Vietnam a Communist government has set out deliberately to conquer a sovereign people in a neighboring state. And to achieve its end, it has used every resource of its own government to carry out its carefully planned program of concealed aggression. North Vietnam's commitment to seize control of the south is no less total than was the commitment of the regime in North Korea in 1950. . . .

This report is a summary of the massive evidence of North Vietnamese aggression obtained by the Government of South Vietnam. . . .

The evidence shows that the hard core of the communist forces attacking South Vietnam were trained in the north and ordered into the south by Hanoi. It shows that the key leadership of the Vietcong (VC), the officers and much of the cadre, many of the technicians, political organizers, and propagandists have come from the north and operate under Hanoi's direction. . . .

The evidence shows that many of the weapons and much of the ammunition and other supplies used by the Vietcong have been sent into South Vietnam from Hanoi. . . . Communist China and other Communist states have been the prime suppliers of these weapons and ammunition, and they have been channeled primarily through North Vietnam.

The directing force behind the effort to conquer South Vietnam is the Communist Party in the North, the Lao Dong (Workers) Party. As in every Communist state, the party is an integral part of the regime itself. North Vietnamese officials have expressed their firm determination to absorb South Vietnam into the Communist world. . . .

I. HANOI SUPPLIES THE KEY PERSONNEL FOR THE ARMED AGGRESSION AGAINST SOUTH VIETNAM

The hard core of the Communist forces attacking South Vietnam are men trained in North Vietnam. They are ordered into the south and remain under the military discipline of the Military High Command in Hanoi. . . . Increasingly the forces sent into the South are native North Vietnamese who have never seen South Vietnam. . . .

Since 1959, nearly 20,000 VC officers, soldiers, and technicians are known to have entered South Vietnam under orders from Hanoi. . . .

It is true that many of the lower level elements of the VC forces are recruited within South Vietnam. However, the thousands of reported cases of VC kidnappings and terrorism make it abundantly clear that threats and other pressures by the Vietcong play a major part in such recruitment. . . .

V. A BRIEF HISTORY OF HANOI'S CAMPAIGN OF AGGRESSION AGAINST SOUTH VIETNAM

While negotiating an end to the Indochina War in Geneva in 1954, the Communists were making plans to take over all former French territory in Southeast Asia. When Vietnam was partitioned, thousands of carefully selected party members were ordered to remain in place in the south and keep their secret apparatus intact to help promote Hanoi's cause. Arms and ammunition were stored away for future use. Guerrilla fighters rejoined their families to await the party's call. Others withdrew to remote jungle and mountain hideouts. The majority—an estimated 90,000—were moved to North Vietnam.

Hanoi's original calculation was that all of Vietnam would fall under its control without resort to force. For this purpose, Communist cadres were ordered to penetrate official and non-official agencies, to propagandize and sow confusion, and generally to use all means short of open violence to aggravate war-torn conditions and to weaken South Vietnam's Government and social fabric.

South Vietnam's refusal to fall in with Hanoi's scheme for peaceful takeover came as a heavy blow to the Communists. Meantime, the Government had stepped up efforts to blunt Vietcong subversion and to expose Communist agents. . . .

The military and insurgency situation was complicated by a quite separate internal political struggle in South Vietnam, which led in November 1963 to the removal of the Diem government and its replacement with a new one. . . . There have been a number of changes in the leadership and composition of the Government in Saigon in the ensuing period.

These internal developments and distractions gave the Vietcong an invaluable opportunity, and they took advantage of it. . . . In the countryside the communists consolidated their hold over some areas and enlarged their military and political apparatus by increased infiltration. . . .

In 1964, 436 South Vietnamese hamlet chiefs and other Government officials were killed outright by the Vietcong and 1,131 were kidnapped. More than 1,350 civilians were killed in bombings and other acts of sabotage. And at least 8,400 civilians were kidnapped by the Vietcong. . . .

Until the regime in Hanoi decides to halt its intervention in the south or until effective steps are taken to maintain peace and security in the area, the Governments of South Vietnam and the United States will continue necessary measures of defense against the Communist armed aggression coming from North Vietnam.

VI. CONCLUSION

. . . The record is conclusive. It establishes beyond question that North Vietnam is carrying out a carefully conceived plan of aggression against the South. . . . It proves that Hanoi continues to press its systematic program of armed aggression into South Vietnam. This aggression violates the United Nations Charter. It is directly contrary to the Geneva Accords of 1954 . . . to which North Vietnam is a party. It shatters the peace of Southeast Asia. It is a fundamental threat to the freedom and security of South Vietnam.

The people of South Vietnam have chosen to resist this threat. At their request, the United States has taken its place beside them in their defensive struggle. . . .

Source: Aggression From the North: The Record of North Vietnam's Campaign to Conquer South Vietnam, U.S. Department of State Publication 7839, Far Eastern Series 130, Washington, D.C., February 1965.

PRESIDENT JOHNSON:
THE JOHNS HOPKINS UNIVERSITY SPEECH
April 7, 1965

Viet-Nam is far away from this quiet campus. We have no territory there, nor do we seek any. The war is dirty and brutal and difficult. And some 400 young men, born into an America that is bursting with opportunity and promise, have ended their lives on Viet-Nam's steaming soil.

Why must we take this painful road?

Why must this Nation hazard its ease, and its interest, and its power for the sake of a people so far away?

We fight because we must fight if we are to live in a world where every country can shape its own destiny. And only in such a world will our own freedom be finally secure. . . .

The first reality is that North Viet-Nam has attacked the independent nation of South Viet-Nam. Its object is total conquest.

Of course, some of the people of South Viet-Nam are participating in the attack on their own government. But trained men and supplies, orders and arms, flow in a constant stream from north to south. . . .

Over this war—and all Asia—is another reality: the deepening shadow of Communist China. The rulers in Hanoi are urged on by Peking. This is a regime which has destroyed freedom in Tibet, which has attacked India, and has been condemned by the United Nations for aggression in Korea. It is a nation which is helping the forces of violence in almost every continent. The contest in Viet-Nam is part of a wider pattern of aggressive purposes. . . .

Why are we in South Viet-Nam? *We are there because we have a promise to keep.* Since 1954 every American President has offered support to the people of South Viet-Nam. . . .

We are also there to strengthen world order. Around the globe, from Berlin to Thailand, are people whose well-being rests, in part, on the belief that they can count on us if they are attacked. To leave Viet-Nam to its fate would shake the confidence of all these people. . . .

We are also there because there are great stakes in the balance. Let no one think for a moment that retreat from Viet-Nam would bring an end to conflict. The battle would be renewed in one country and then another. The central lesson of our time is that the appetite of aggression is never satisfied. . . .

Our objective is the independence of South Viet-Nam, and its freedom from attack. We want nothing for ourselves—only that the people of South Viet-Nam be allowed to guide their own country in their own way. . . .

These countries of southeast Asia are homes for millions of impoverished people. . . .

For our part I will ask the Congress to join in a billion dollar American investment. . . .

The task is nothing less than to enrich the hopes and existence of more than a hundred million people. And there is much to be done.

The vast Mekong River can provide food and water and power on a scale to dwarf even our own TVA. . . .

Every night before I turn out the lights to sleep I ask myself this question: Have I done everything that I can do to unite this country? Have I done everything I can to help unite the world, to try to bring peace and hope to all the peoples of the world? Have I done enough?. . .

This generation of the world must choose: destroy or build, kill or aid, hate or understand. . . .

Source: United States Government, *Public Papers of the Presidents of the United States: Lyndon B. Johnson, 1965* (Washington, 1967), pp. 394–99.

LIN BIAO, "ON PEOPLE'S WAR"
1965

Ours is the epoch in which world capitalism and imperialism are heading for their doom and socialism and communism are marching to victory. Comrade Mao Zedong's theory of people's war is not only a product of the Chinese revolution. . . . The new experience gained in people's revolutionary struggles in various countries since World War II has provided continuous evidence that Mao Zedong's thought is a common asset of the revolutionary people of the whole world. . . .

Since World War II, U.S. imperialism has stepped into the shoes of German, Japanese, and Italian fascism and has been trying to build a great American empire. . . . It is the most rabid aggressor in human history. . . .

Today, the conditions are more favorable than ever before for the waging of people's wars by the revolutionary peoples of Asia, Africa, and Latin America against U.S. imperialism and its lackeys. . . . The whole capitalist-imperialist system has become drastically weaker and is in the process of increasing convulsion and disintegration. . . .

When committing aggression in a foreign country, U.S. imperialism can only employ part of its forces, which are sent to fight an unjust war far from their native land and therefore have a low morale. . . .

Everything is divisible. And so is this colossus of U.S. imperialism. It can be split up and defeated. The peoples of Asia, Africa, Latin America and other regions can destroy it piece by piece. . . . That is why the greatest fear of U.S. imperialism is that people's wars will be launched in different parts of the world.

Vietnam is the most convincing current example of a victim of aggression defeating U.S. imperialism by a people's war. The United States has made South Vietnam a testing ground for suppression of people's war. It has carried on this experiment for many years, and everybody can now see that the U.S. aggressors are unable to find a way of coping with people's war. . . . The Vietnamese people have brought the power of people's war into full play in their struggle against the U.S. aggressors. The U.S. aggressors are in danger of being swamped in the people's war in Vietnam. They are deeply worried that their defeat in Vietnam will lead to a chain reaction. . . . The more they expand the war, the heavier will be their fall and the more disastrous their defeat. The people in other parts of the world will see still more clearly that U.S. imperialism can be defeated, and that what the Vietnamese people can do, they can do too. . . .

Source: U.S. Senate, Committee on Foreign Relations, *Background Information Relating to Southeast Asia and Vietnam,* 91st Congress, 2nd Session, Washington, D.C., 1970.

THE BREZHNEV DOCTRINE
September 1968

In connection with the events in Czechoslovakia, the question of the relationship and inter-connection between the socialist countries' national interests and their internationalist obligations has assumed particular urgency and sharpness. The measures taken jointly by the Soviet Union and other socialist countries to defend the socialist gains of the Czechoslovak people are of enormous significance for strengthening the socialist commonwealth, which is the main achievement of the international working class.

At the same time it is impossible to ignore the allegations . . . that the actions of the five socialist countries contradict the Marxist-Leninist principle of sovereignty and the right of nations to self-determination.

Such arguments are untenable primarily because they are based on an abstract, non-class approach to the question of sovereignty and the right of nations to self-determination.

There is no doubt that the peoples of the socialist countries and the Communist parties have and must have freedom to determine their country's path of development. However, any decision of theirs must damage neither socialism in their own country, nor the fundamental interests of the other socialist countries, nor the world-wide workers' movement. . . . This means that every Communist party is responsible not only to its own people but also to all the socialist countries and to the entire Communist movement. Whoever forgets this is placing sole emphasis on the autonomy and independence of Communist parties. . . .

Each Communist party is free to apply the principles of Marxism-Leninism and socialism in its own country, but it cannot deviate from these principles. . . .

The weakening of any link in the world socialist system has a direct effect on all the socialist countries, which cannot be indifferent. Thus, the antisocialist forces in Czechoslovakia were in essence using talk about the right to self-determination to cover up demands for so-called neutrality and . . . withdrawal from the socialist commonwealth. But implementation of such "self-determination," i.e., Czechoslovakia's separation from the socialist commonwealth, would run counter to Czechoslovakia's fundamental interests and would harm the other socialist countries. . . .

Source: S. Kovalev article, *Pravda*, September 26, 1968, in *Problems of Communism*, Nov./Dec. 1968, vol. 17, p. 25.

VIII

THE NIXON AND FORD ADMINISTRATIONS

95

THE NIXON DOCTRINE
November 1969

. . .Let me briefly explain what has been described as the Nixon Doctrine—a policy which not only will help end the war in Vietnam but which is an essential element of our program to prevent future Vietnams. . . .

- First, the United States will keep all of its treaty commitments.
- Second, we shall provide a shield if a nuclear power threatens the freedom of a nation allied with us or of a nation whose survival we consider vital to our security.
- Third, in cases involving other types of aggression, we shall furnish military and economic assistance when requested in accordance with our treaty commitments. But we shall look to the nation directly threatened to assume the primary responsibility of providing the manpower for its defense. . . .

The defense of freedom is everybody's business—not just America's business. And it is particularly the responsibility of the people whose freedom is threatened. . . .

Source: Department of State, *Bulletin,* November 24, 1969.

NIXON'S EXPLANATION OF
THE INVASION OF CAMBODIA
April 30, 1970

. . .In cooperation with the armed forces of South Vietnam, attacks are being launched this week to clean out major enemy sanctuaries on the Cambodian-Vietnam border. . . .

Tonight American and South Vietnamese units will attack the . . . key control center [that] has been occupied by the North Vietnamese and Vietcong for five years in blatant violation of Cambodia's neutrality.

This is not an invasion of Cambodia. The areas in which these attacks will be launched are completely occupied and controlled by North Vietnamese forces. Our purpose is not to occupy the areas. Once enemy forces are driven out of these sanctuaries and once their military supplies are destroyed, we will withdraw. . . .

We take this action not for the purpose of expanding the war into Cambodia, but for the purpose of ending the war in Vietnam and winning the just peace we all desire. . . .

Let us look again at the record. We have stopped the bombing of North Vietnam. . . . We have announced withdrawal of over 250,000 of our men. We have offered to withdraw all of our men, if they will withdraw theirs. . . .

The action that I have announced tonight puts the leaders of North Vietnam on notice that we will be patient in working for peace, we will be conciliatory at the conference table, but we will not be humiliated. We will not be defeated. We will not allow American men by the thousands to be killed by an enemy from privileged sanctuaries. . . .

If, when the chips are down, the world's most powerful nation, the United States of America, acts like a pitiful, helpless giant, the forces of totalitarianism and anarchy will threaten free nations and free institutions throughout the world. . . .

During my campaign for the Presidency, I pledged to bring Americans home from Vietnam. They are coming home.

I promised to end this war. I shall keep that promise.

I promised to win a just peace. I shall keep that promise. . . .

I have rejected all political considerations in making this decision. . . . Whether I may be a one-term President is insignificant compared to whether by our failure to act in this crisis the United States proves itself unworthy to lead the forces of freedom in this critical period in world history. . . .

Source: Department of State, *Bulletin*, May 18, 1970.

JOINT STATEMENT ISSUED BY PRESIDENT NIXON AND PREMIER ZHOU ENLAI
February 1972

President Richard Nixon of the United States of America visited the People's Republic of China at the invitation of Premier Chou En-lai of the People's Republic of China from February 21 to February 28, 1972. . . .

There are essential differences between China and the United States in their social systems and foreign policies. However, the two sides agreed that countries, regardless of their social systems, should conduct their relations on the principles of respect for the sovereignty and territorial integrity of all states, non-aggression against other states, non-interference in the internal affairs of other states, equality and mutual benefit, and peaceful coexistence. International disputes should be settled on this basis, without resorting to the use or threat of force. . . .

The two sides reviewed the long-standing serious disputes between China and the United States. The Chinese side reaffirmed its position: The Taiwan question is the crucial question obstructing the normalization of relations between China and the United States; the Government of the People's Republic of China is the sole legal government of China; Taiwan is a province of China which has long been returned to the motherland; the liberation of Taiwan is China's internal affair in which no other country has the right to interfere; and all U.S. forces and military installations must be withdrawn from Taiwan. The Chinese Government firmly opposes any activities which aim at the creation of "one Taiwan" or advocate that "the status of Taiwan remains to be determined."

The U.S. side declared: The United States acknowledges that all Chinese on either side of the Taiwan Strait maintain there is but one China and that Taiwan is a part of China. The United States Government does not challenge that position. It reaffirms its interest in a peaceful settlement of the Taiwan question by the Chinese themselves. With this prospect in mind, it affirms the ultimate objective of the withdrawal of all U.S. forces and military installations from Taiwan. In the meantime, it will progressively reduce its forces and military installations on Taiwan as the tension in the area diminishes. . . .

Both sides view bilateral trade as another area from which mutual benefit can be derived, and agreed that economic relations based on equality and mutual benefit are in the interest of the peoples of the two countries. They agree to facilitate the progressive development of trade between their two countries. . . .

Source: Joint Communiqué issued at Shanghai, February 27, 1972. U.S. Department of State *Bulletin*, March 20, 1972, pp. 435-38.

THE HELSINKI ACCORDS
August 1975

I. SOVEREIGN EQUALITY, RESPECT FOR THE RIGHTS INHERENT IN SOVEREIGNTY

The participating States will respect each other's sovereign equality and individuality as well as all the rights inherent in and encompassed by its sovereignty, including in particular the right of every State to juridical equality, to territorial integrity and to freedom and political independence. They will also respect each other's right freely to choose and develop its political, social, economic and cultural systems as well as its right to determine its laws and regulations. . . .

II. REFRAINING FROM THE THREAT OR USE OF FORCE

The participating States will refrain in their mutual relations, as well as in their international relations in general, from the threat or use of force against the territorial integrity or political independence of any State, or in any other manner inconsistent with the purpose of the United Nations and with the present Declaration. . . .

III. INVIOLABILITY OF FRONTIERS

The participating States regard as inviolable all one another's frontiers as well as the frontiers of all States in Europe. . . .

VI. NON-INTERVENTION IN INTERNAL AFFAIRS

The participating States will refrain from any intervention, direct or indirect, individual or collective, in the internal or external affairs falling within the domestic jurisdiction of another participating State. . . .

They will accordingly refrain from any form of armed intervention or threat of such intervention against another participating State. . . .

VII. RESPECT FOR HUMAN RIGHTS AND FUNDAMENTAL FREEDOMS, INCLUDING THE FREEDOM OF THOUGHT, CONSCIENCE, RELIGION OR BELIEF

The participating states will respect human rights and fundamental freedoms, including the freedom of thought, conscience, religion or belief, for all without distinction as to race, sex, language or religion.

They will promote and encourage the effective exercise of civil, political, economic, social, cultural and other rights and freedoms of all which derive from the inherent dignity of the human person and are essential for his free and full development.

Within this framework the participating States will recognize and respect the freedom of the individual to profess and practice, alone or in community with others, religion, or belief, acting in accordance with the dictates of his own conscience. . . .

In the field of human rights and fundamental freedoms, the participating States will act in conformity with the purposes and principles of the Charter of the United Nations and with the Universal Declaration of Human Rights. They will also fulfill their obligations as set forth in the international declarations and agreements in this field, including inter alia the International Covenants on Human Rights, by which they may be bound.

Source: Conference on Security and Cooperation in Europe: Final Act, Aug. 1, 1975, U.S. Department of State, *Bulletin*, Sept. 1, 1975, pp. 324–25.

IX

THE CARTER ADMINISTRATION

JOINT U.S.-PRC STATEMENT ESTABLISHING DIPLOMATIC RELATIONS, 1979

The United States of America and the People's Republic of China have agreed to recognize each other and to establish diplomatic relations as of January 1, 1979.

The United States of America recognizes the Government of the People's Republic of China as the sole legal Government of China. Within this context, the people of the United States will maintain cultural, commercial, and other unofficial relations with the people of Taiwan. . . .

The Government of the United States of America acknowledges the Chinese position that there is but one China and Taiwan is part of China. . . .

Source: Joint Communiqué on the Establishment of Diplomatic Relations Between the United States of America and the People's Republic of China, December 15, 1978, U.S. Department of State, *Bulletin*, January 1, 1979, p. 25.

TAIWAN RELATIONS ACT, 1979

. . .

Sec. 2

(a) The President having terminated governmental relations between the United States and the governing authorities on Taiwan recognized by the United States as the Republic of China prior to January 1, 1979, the Congress finds that the enactment of this Act is necessary—
   (1) to help maintain peace, security, and stability in the western Pacific; and
   (2) to promote the foreign policy of the United States by authorizing the continuation of commercial, cultural, and other relations between the people of the United States and the people on Taiwan.

(b) It is the policy of the United States—
   (1) to preserve and promote extensive, close, and friendly commercial, cultural, and other relations between the people of the United States and the people on Taiwan, as well as the people on the China mainland. . .;
   (2) to declare that peace and stability in the area are in the political, security, and economic interests of the United States. . .;
   (3) to make clear that the United States' decision to establish diplomatic relations with the People's Republic of China rests upon the expectation that the future of Taiwan will be determined by peaceful means;
   (4) to consider any effort to determine the future of Taiwan by other than peaceful means, including by boycotts or embargoes, a threat to the peace and security of the western Pacific area and of grave concern to the United States;
   (5) to provide Taiwan with arms of a defensive character; and
   (6) to maintain the capacity of the United States to resist any resort to force or other forms of coercion that would jeopardize the security, or the social or economic system, of the people on Taiwan. . . .

Source: Taiwan Relations Act (Public Law 96-8), April 10, 1979, *Statutes At Large,* Washington, D.C., 1981, Vol. 93, pp. 14–16.

‾IAN-ISRAELI PEACE TREATY
March 1979

...c Arab Republic of Egypt and the Government of the State of Israel:

PREAMBLE

Reaffirming their adherence to the "Framework for Peace in the Middle East Agreed at Camp David," dated September 17, 1978;. . .

Agree to the following provisions in the free exercise of their sovereignty. . .:

Article I

1. The state of war between the Parties will be terminated and peace will be established between them upon the exchange of instruments of ratification of this Treaty.
2. Israel will withdraw all its armed forces and civilians from the Sinai behind the international boundary between Egypt and mandated Palestine, . . . and Egypt will resume the exercise of its full sovereignty over the Sinai.
3. . . . The Parties will establish normal and friendly relations. . . .

Article III

1. The Parties . . . will refrain from the threat or use of force, directly or indirectly, against each other and will settle all disputes between them by peaceful means. . . .

Article V

1. . . . Israeli nationals, vessels and cargoes, as well as persons, vessels and cargoes destined for or coming from Israel, shall be accorded non-discriminatory treatment in all matters connected with use of the [Suez] Canal.
2. The Parties consider the Strait of Tiran and the Gulf of Aqaba to be international waterways open to all nations for unimpeded and non-suspendable freedom of navigation and overflight. . . .

Article VI

. . .

4. The Parties undertake not to enter into any obligations in conflict with this Treaty.
5. . . . In the event of a conflict between the obligations of the Parties under the present Treaty and any of their other obligations, the obligations under this Treaty will be binding and implemented. . . .

For the Government of the Arab Republic of Egypt: *Anwar Sadat*
For the Government of Israel: *Menachem Begin*
Witnessed by: *Jimmy Carter*
President of the United States of America

Source: Treaty of Peace Between Arab Republic of Egypt and the State of Israel, March 26, 1979, U.S. Department of State, *Selected Documents No. 11,* Washington, D.C., Bureau of Public Affairs, April 1979, pp. 1–3.

THE CARTER DOCTRINE
January 24, 1980

"An attempt by any outside force to gain control of the Persian Gulf region will be regarded as an assault on the vital interests of the United States of America, and such an assault will be repelled by use of any means necessary, including military force."

Source: President Jimmy Carter's State of The Union Address before Congress, January 23, 1980, *Presidential Papers: Jimmy Carter,* 1980-81, pp. 194–99.

X

REAGAN, BUSH, AND THE FINAL PHASES OF THE COLD WAR

PRESIDENT REAGAN:
GOALS OF THE SOVIET UNION
January 29, 1981

Q. Mr. President, what do you see as the long-range intentions of the Soviet Union? Do you think, for instance, the Kremlin is bent on world domination, . . . or do you think that under other circumstances détente is possible?

The President. Well, so far détente's been a one-way street that the Soviet Union has used to pursue its own aims. I don't have to think of an answer as to what I think their intentions are; they have repeated it. I know of no leader of the Soviet Union since the revolution, and including the present leadership, that has not more than once repeated in the various Communist congresses they hold their determination that their goal must be the promotion of world revolution and a one-world Socialist or Communist state. . . .

Now, as long as they do that and as long as they, at the same time, have openly and publicly declared that the only morality they recognize is what will further their cause, meaning they reserve unto themselves the right to commit any crime, to lie, to cheat, in order to attain that, and that is moral, not immoral, and we operate on a different set of standards, I think when you do business with them, even at a détente, you keep that in mind.

Source: President Ronald Reagan, News Conference, Jan. 29, 1981, *Presidential Papers: Administration of Ronald Reagan.*

REMARKS BY PRESIDENT REAGAN AND GENERAL SECRETARY GORBACHEV, WASHINGTON SUMMIT
December 1987

PRESIDENT REAGAN

The greatest accomplishment of these 3 days was the signing of a treaty to eliminate a whole class of U.S. and Soviet nuclear weapons. . . . We have begun the task of actually reducing these deadly weapons, rather than simply putting limits on their growth.

The INF [Intermediate-Range Nuclear Forces] Treaty, as proud of it as we are, should be viewed as a beginning, not an end. Further arms reduction is now possible. I am pleased some progress has been made toward a strategic arms reduction treaty over the last 3 days. . . .

GENERAL SECRETARY GORBACHEV

. . . A good deal has been accomplished. I would like to emphasize in particular an unprecedented step in the history of the nuclear age: the signing of the treaty under which the two militarily and strategically greatest powers have assumed an obligation to actually destroy a portion of their nuclear weapons, thus, we hope, setting in motion the process of nuclear disarmament.

In our talks with President Ronald Reagan, some headway has been made on the central issue of that process, achieving substantial reductions of strategic offensive arms which are the most potent weapons in the world. . . .

I believe that what we have accomplished during the meeting and the discussions will, with time, help considerably to improve the atmosphere in the world at large and in America itself in terms of its more correct and tolerant perception of my country, the Soviet Union.

Today, the Soviet Union and the United States are closer to the common goal of strengthening international security. . . .

Source: Departure Remarks of President Reagan and General Secretary Gorbachev at Conclusion of the Washington Summit, December 10, 1987, U.S. Department of State, *Bulletin,* February 1988, pp. 16–18.

THE BOLAND AMENDMENT
1983

TITLE VIII—PROHIBITION ON COVERT ASSISTANCE FOR MILITARY OPERATIONS IN NICARAGUA; AUTHORIZATION OF OVERT INTERDICTION ASSISTANCE

PROHIBITION ON COVERT ASSISTANCE FOR MILITARY OPERATIONS IN NICARAGUA

Sec. 801. (a) None of the funds appropriated for fiscal year 1983 or 1984 for the Central Intelligence Agency or any other department, agency, or entity of the United States involved in intelligence activities may be obligated or expended for . . . supporting, directly or indirectly, military or paramilitary operations in Nicaragua by any nation, group, organization, movement, or individual. . . .

Source: Boland Amendment concerning U.S. Military and paramilitary operations in Nicaragua, U.S. Congress, Committee on Foreign Affairs, *98th Congress, 1st Session,* Washington, D.C.: Government Printing Office, 1983, pp. 83–84.

IRAN-CONTRA: THE FINAL REPORT
August 1993

EXECUTIVE SUMMARY

In October and November 1986, two secret U.S. Government operations were publicly exposed, potentially implicating Reagan Administration officials in illegal activities. These operations were the provision of assistance to the military activities of the Nicaraguan contra rebels during an October 1984 to October 1986 prohibition on such aid, and the sale of U.S. arms to Iran in contravention of stated U.S. policy and in possible violation of arms-export controls. In late November 1986, Reagan Administration officials announced that some of the proceeds from the sale of U.S. arms to Iran had been diverted to the contras. . . .

OVERALL CONCLUSIONS

The investigations and prosecutions have shown that high-ranking Administration officials violated laws and executive orders in the Iran/contra matter.

Independent Counsel concluded that:

- the sales of arms to Iran contravened United States Government policy and may have violated the Arms Export Control Act;
- the provision and coordination of support to the contras violated the Boland Amendment ban on aid to military activities in Nicaragua;
- the policies behind both the Iran and contra operations were fully reviewed and developed at the highest levels of the Reagan Administration;
- although there was little evidence of National Security Council level knowledge of most of the actual contra-support operations, there was no evidence that any NSC member dissented from the underlying policy—keeping the contras alive despite congressional limitations on contra support;
- the Iran operations were carried out with the knowledge of, among others, President Ronald Reagan, Vice President George Bush, Secretary of State George P. Shultz, Secretary of Defense Caspar W. Weinberger, Director of Central Intelligence William J. Casey, and national security advisers Robert C. McFarlane and John M. Poindexter; of these officials, only Weinberger and Shultz dissented from the policy decision, and Weinberger eventually acquiesced by ordering the Department of Defense to provide the necessary arms;
- large volumes of highly relevant, contemporaneously created documents were systematically and willfully withheld from investigators by several Reagan Administration officials;

- following the revelation of these operations in October and November 1986, Reagan Administration officials deliberately deceived the Congress and the public about the level and extent of official knowledge of and support for these operations.

In addition, Independent Counsel concluded that the off-the-books nature of the Iran and contra operations gave line-level personnel the opportunity to commit money crimes. . . .

THE BASIC FACTS OF IRAN/CONTRA

The Iran/contra affair concerned two secret Reagan Administration policies whose operations were coordinated by National Security Council staff. The Iran operation involved efforts in 1985 and 1986 to obtain the release of Americans held hostage in the Middle East through the sale of U.S. weapons to Iran, despite an embargo on such sales. The contra operations from 1984 through most of 1986 involved the secret governmental support of contra military and paramilitary activities in Nicaragua, despite congressional prohibition of this support.

The Iran and contra operations were merged when funds generated from the sale of weapons to Iran were diverted to support the contra effort in Nicaragua. Although this "diversion" may be the most dramatic aspect of Iran/contra, it is important to emphasize that both the Iran and contra operations, separately, violated United States policy and law. The ignorance of the "diversion" asserted by President Reagan and his Cabinet officers on the National Security Council in no way absolves them of responsibility for the underlying Iran and contra operations. . . . The exposure of the Iran/contra affair generated a new round of illegality. Beginning with the testimony of Elliott Abrams and others in October 1986 and continuing through the public testimony of Caspar W. Weinberger on the last day of the congressional hearings in the summer of 1987, senior Reagan Administration officials engaged in a concerted effort to deceive Congress and the public about their knowledge of the support for the operations.

Independent Counsel has concluded that the President's most senior advisers and the Cabinet members on the National Security Council participated in the strategy to make National Security staff members McFarlane, Poindexter and North the scapegoats whose sacrifice would protect the Reagan Administration in its final two years. In an important sense, this strategy succeeded. Independent Counsel discovered much of the best evidence of the cover-up in the final year of active investigation, too late for most prosecutions. . . .

THE WHITE HOUSE AND OFFICE OF THE VICE PRESIDENT

As the White House section of this report describes in detail, the investigation found no credible evidence that President Reagan violated any criminal statute. The OIC could not prove that Reagan authorized or was aware of the diversion or that he had knowledge of the extent of North's control of the contra-resupply network. Nevertheless, he set the stage for the illegal activities of others by encouraging and, in general terms, ordering support of the contras during the October 1984 to October 1986 period when funds for the contras were cut off by the Boland Amendment, and in authorizing the sale of arms to Iran, in contravention of the U.S. embargo on such sales. The President's disregard for civil laws enacted to limit presidential actions abroad—specifically the Boland Amendment, the

Arms Export Control Act and congressional-notification requirements in covert-action laws—created a climate in which some of the Government officers assigned to implement his policies felt emboldened to circumvent such laws. . . .

Independent Counsel's investigation did not develop evidence that proved that Vice President Bush violated any criminal statute. Contrary to his public pronouncements, however, he was fully aware of the Iran arms sales. Bush was regularly briefed, along with the President, on the Iran arms sales, and he participated in discussions to obtain third-country support for the contras. . . .

OBSERVATIONS AND CONCLUSIONS

This report concludes with Independent Counsel's observations and conclusions. He observes that the governmental problems presented by Iran/Contra are not those of rogue operations, but rather those of Executive Branch efforts to evade congressional oversight. As this report documents, the competing roles of the attorney general—adviser to the President and top law enforcement officer—come into irreconcilable conflict in the case of high-level Executive Branch wrongdoing. Independent Counsel concludes that congressional oversight alone cannot correct the deficiencies that result when an attorney general abandons the law-enforcement responsibilities of that office and undertakes, instead, to protect the President. . . .

Source: Final Report of the Independent Counsel [Lawrence E. Walsh] for Iran/Contra Matters submitted to Judge David Sentelle, Division for the Purpose of Appointing Independent Counsels, U.S. Court of Appeals for District of Columbia, Washington, D.C., pp. xiii–xxv, August 1993.

CONVENTIONAL FORCES IN EUROPE (CFE)
November 1990

WHITE HOUSE FACT SHEET

Today the 22 members of NATO and the Warsaw Pact signed a landmark agreement limiting conventional armed forces in Europe (CFE). The CFE treaty will establish parity in major conventional armaments between East and West in Europe from the Atlantic to the Urals. The treaty will limit the size of the Soviet forces to about one third of the total armaments permitted to all the countries in Europe. The treaty includes an unprecedented monitoring regime, including detailed information exchange, on-site inspection, challenge inspection, and monitoring of destruction.

East-West Limits

The treaty sets equal ceilings from the Atlantic to the Urals on key armaments essential for conducting surprise attack and initiating large-scale offensive operations. . . .

Large amounts of equipment will be destroyed to meet the obligations of the CFE treaty. The Soviet Union alone will be obliged to destroy thousands of weapons, much more equipment than will be reduced by all the NATO countries combined. NATO will meet its destruction obligations by destroying its oldest equipment. . . .

The treaty includes unprecedented provisions for detailed information exchanges, on-site inspections, challenge inspections, and on-site monitoring of destruction. . . . Parties have an unlimited right to monitor the process of destruction. . . .

Text of the Joint Declaration of Twenty-Two States
November 19, 1990

The Heads of State or Government of Belgium, Bulgaria, Canada, the Czech and Slovak Federal Republic, Denmark, France, Germany, Greece, Hungary, Iceland, Italy, Luxembourg, the Netherlands, Norway, Poland, Portugal, Romania, Spain, Turkey, the Union of Soviet Socialist Republics, the United Kingdom and the United States of America

- greatly welcoming the historic changes in Europe,
- gratified by the growing implementation throughout Europe of a common commitment to pluralist democracy, the rule of law and human rights, which are essential to lasting security on the continent,
- affirming the end of the era of division and confrontation which has lasted for more than four decades, . . .

Issue the following Declaration:

1. The signatories solemnly declare that, in the new era of European relations which is beginning, they are no longer adversaries. . . .
2. They recall their obligations under the Charter of the United Nations and reaffirm all of their commitments under the Helsinki Final Act. . . .
3. They recognize that security is indivisible and that the security of each of their countries is inextricably linked to the security of all. . . .

Source: Treaty on Conventional Armed Forces in Europe, November 19, 1990, *Weekly Compilation of Presidential Documents:* 1990, pp. 1868–72.

"THE FAILURE OF OUR SUCCESS"
George F. Kennan
February 15, 1994

The Council on Foreign Relations in New York City held a party for the diplomat and author George F. Kennan in celebration of his 90th birthday on Feb. 15. His remarks, excerpted, follow.

I am reminded that it was 47 years ago that my involvement with the Council on Foreign Relations began in earnest. At the end of 1946, I had attended and addressed, in this very room, a dinner at which I spoke about the Russia of that day. This led to a further meeting in January, this time with the Council's newly established Discussion Group on Soviet Foreign Policy.

It was shortly thereafter that Ham Armstrong, as editor of *Foreign Affairs,* wrote to me, asking me to set forth in an article for that journal the gist of what I had been saying on these occasions about Russia and Soviet-American relations.

Now, Ham Armstrong was a great and talented seducer of victims from whom he hoped to extract a useful article. This was not the last one he would extract from me over the years. I was no more able to resist these extraordinary allures than were many others. What came out of this approach was what became known as the "X" article. And this was the beginning of my life of sin as a participant in the public discussion of Soviet-American relations.

Now first, a word or two from the perspective of 47 intervening years, about what was being discussed at those early meetings. What I was then advocating for our Government was a policy of "containment" of Soviet expansionist pressures, a policy aimed at halting the expansion of Soviet power into Central and Western Europe.

I viewed this as primarily a diplomatic and political task, though not wholly without military implications. I considered that if and when we had succeeded in persuading the Soviet leadership that the continuation of these expansionist pressures not only held out for them no hopes for success but would be, in many respects, to their disadvantage, then the moment would have come for serious talks with them about the future of Europe.

But when, some three years later, this moment had arrived—when we had made our point with the Marshall Plan, with the successful resistance to the Berlin blockade and other measures—when the lesson I wanted to see us convey to Moscow had been successfully conveyed, then it was one of the great disappointments of my life to discover that neither our Government nor our Western European allies had any interest in entering into such discussions at all. What they and the others wanted from Moscow, with respect to the future of Europe, was essentially "unconditional surrender." They were prepared to wait for it. And this was the beginning of the 40 years of cold war.

Those of my opponents of that day who have survived into the present age would say, I am sure: "You see. We were right. The collapse of the Soviet system amounted to the unconditional surrender we envisaged—an involuntary one if you will, but surrender nevertheless. And we paid nothing for it."

To which I should have to reply: "But we did pay a great deal for it. We paid with 40 years of enormous and otherwise unnecessary military expenditures. We paid through the cultivation of nuclear weaponry to the point where the vast and useless nuclear arsenals had become (and remain today) a danger to the very environment of the planet. And we paid with 40 years of Communist control in Eastern Germany, Czechoslovakia and Hungary, the damages of which to the structure of civilization in those countries we are only now beginning to observe. We paid all of this because we were too timid to negotiate."

We will never know who was right and who was wrong in this disagreement. The one course was tried. Its consequences, good and bad, are now visible. The other course remained hypothetical. Its results will never be known.

We are now in a new age. It is an age which, for all its confusions and dangers, is marked by one major blessing: for the first time in centuries, there are no great-power rivalries that threaten immediately the peace of the world. We must do all in our power to see that things remain this way. But aside from that one encouraging situation, what we see is a highly unsettled and unstable world—a world full of squabbles, conflicts and violent encounters, some not without dangers to world peace and stability.

This presents a challenge for which we are poorly prepared. For over 60 years, the attention of our policy makers and public opinion was monopolized by the effort to respond to what appeared to be, and sometimes were, great and overriding dangers—the Nazis, the Japanese militarists, then Stalin's Russia.

Our statesmen and our public are unaccustomed to reacting to a world situation that offers no such great and all-absorbing focal points for American policy. And it is not surprising that we should now be hearing demands for some sort of a single grand strategy of foreign policy, to replace our fixation on the Soviet Union, and to serve as a guide for our responses to all those troublesome situations.

And about this demand, coming to us from many quarters, there are one or two things I think we ought to note.

First of all, as a problem for American statesmanship, this present situation is not really all that new. Similar situations existed in the early years of this Republic, and again toward the end of the 19th century.

And if you could bring to life some of the wiser of the American statesmen of those earlier periods and ask their opinion about the present demands for some sort of a grand strategy with which to meet all our problems, they would say, I suspect, something like the following:

Why do you want anything like that? Yes, of course, your world is complex. So was ours. But many of these troublesome situations that bother you do not really threaten your interests. And even for those that do, there could be no single grand design—no vast common denominator—that would tell you how each of them should be approached. Each has to be judged on its merit. Discard, then, this traditional American fondness for trying to solve problems by putting them into broad categories. What you need are not policies—much less a single policy. What you need are sound principles: principles that accord with the nature, the needs, the interests and the limitations of our country.

Some of these principles seem to be relatively immutable. A number were enunciated by John Quincy Adams in his great Fourth of July speech of 1821, and they have lost none of their relevance. Adams observed that if America should enlist under other banners than her own, "were they even the banners of foreign independence, she would involve herself beyond the power of extrications, in all the wars of interest and intrigue, of individual avarice, envy and ambition, which assume the colors and usurp the standard of freedom."

Principles, too, have of course to be reviewed and adjusted to meet the particular challenges of the time. And if you were to ask what such principles might be today, I could only say: "Look closely at our own society. Look at its strengths and weaknesses, at its successes and failures, at the possibilities and the dangers that confront it.

"And then ask yourselves how such a country ought to shape its foreign relations in such a way as to help it to be what it could be to itself and to its world environment, bearing in mind, of course, that it is primarily by example, never by precept, that a country such as ours exerts the most useful influence beyond its borders, but remembering, too, that there are limits to what any one sovereign country can do to help another, and that unless we preserve the quality, the vigor and the morale of our own society, we will be of little use to anyone at all."

Source: New York Times, Monday, March 14, 1994. Reprinted by permission.